Spiritual Elders

Women of Worth
in the Third Millennium

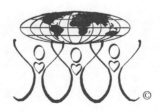

by
Betty Anne Sulliva

D1502751

Brockton Publishing Company
Houston, Texas

Manufactured in the United States of America

ISBN 1-887918-24-8

Library of Congress Catalog Card Number: 98-88768

Book design by B.B.Brown.
Editing by Cathy Schmermund.
Logo concept by Betty Anne Sullivan
Drawings by Mary Hortman
Computer graphics by B.B.Brown
All photographs taken or provided by author unless noted.

Hardware: PowerSpec 6140 computer, Philips Magnavox Monitor,
         Umax Astra 2400 scanner, TI Microlaser Power Pro
         Laser Printer.
Software: Adobe PageMaker® 6.5, Adobe Illustrator® 7.0, and
         Adobe Photoshop® 4.0
Typefaces: Dauphin and Times New Roman, True Type fonts, text
         set at 12/18.

Text and cover printed by Bold Creative Services, Houston, Texas.
Text paper: 60lb. Hammermill offset, white, acid free, recycled.
Cover paper: Springhill 10pt C1S.
Negatives supplied by Imageset, Houston.
All paper supplied by Bosworth Paper, Houston.
Foil work and UV coating by American Embossing, Houston.
Bound by Rasch Graphic Services, Houston.

Brockton Publishing Company
Houston, Texas
1-800-968-7065

This book is dedicated
to my beloved husband
Ivan
whose spirit is indomitable
and whose support is legendary

"Age-ing will find us.
Sage-ing must be sought."

Betty Anne Sullivan

For Jenny,

A spiritual elder and woman of
extraordinary worth with my deepest
respect. Blessings with love,

Betty Anne Sullivan

10-25-03

Acknowledgments

My deep gratitude goes to Zalman Schachter-Shalomi, Ph.D., for his pioneering effort in establishing the Spiritual Eldering Institute (SEI) and the consciousness-raising experiences that I have had at the seminars that he conducted in Boston, Philadelphia and The Omega Institute in Rhinebeck, New York. Reb Zalman is the personification of a sage and, with deep humility, so graciously shares his wisdom.

This book has been greatly enriched by Steffi Shapiro, L.I.C.S.W., and Elizabeth David,M.A., SEI seminar leaders. They are truly my spiritual sisters. We went through the SEI seminar leaders' training program together and for several years, thereafter, did bi-weekly check-ins with each other. Our check-ins included sharing our current consciousness about our minds, our bodies, our emotions and our spirits. Their sharings, and their feedback to me, have significantly enriched my spiritual journey. We team-taught many seminars in New England and their deep spirits blessed each seminar making them most memorable.

June Caldwell, an SEI director, generously reviewed the manuscript and supported this work from the very beginning. She is a very creative listener. Her thoughts are present in this work.

More recently I have team-taught seminars with Judith Helburn, M.L.S., a SEI seminar leader from Austin, Texas. Judith, a new spiritual sister, has written part of the creativity chapter and made valuable suggestions for the text. For this new relationship, and Judith's considerable talent, I am very grateful.

I am also very grateful to my dear sister Joan Ward-Greene, M.S.W., who served as an SEI director. She was a pioneer for senior programs that were established following the enactment of the original Older Americans Act. She was the first person to encourage me to work with elders and generously contributed her support and expertise to the manuscript.

My brother Joe Moriarty, M.B.A., has a great gift for humor that I really admire. The calls of encouragement, from he and his lovely wife, Kristen, were most welcome as they always brought much-needed comic relief.

My sincere appreciation goes to my professional colleague, Donnelle Eargle, Ph.D., for her critical review of the manuscript and her insightful suggestions. Donnelle spent valuable time with me discussing the topics for inclusion in the manuscript.

My special thanks to Florence Ross, an early supporter of the work of the Spiritual Eldering Institute, whose comments on the manuscript have been invaluable and whose encouragement has been there from the very beginning. She is, indeed, a spiritual sage and her presence, as a she-elder and a woman of worth, continues to inspire me.

I would also like to thank the other original SEI seminar leaders Mindy Turin, Carol Jacobs, Rev. Donna O'Keefe, Fred Strugatz, and Joyce Quinlan who worked on the development of the first leader's training curriculum. Each has contributed, in a very special way, to my personal evolvement as a spiritual elder.

Bahira Sugarman and Shaya Isenberg are two very special people. Along with Reb Zalman they have been the faculty that has nurtured the seminar leaders. They are gifted and patient and have supported this work through their strong leadership. In the book I share about the Reiki healing that Bahira performed on me.

Lynne Iser has been the spirit behind the Spiritual Eldering Institute. I want to acknowledge the important role that she has played in its development and thank her for supporting the work of the seminar leaders. She is our communications-central and keeps us informed of the ongoing work of SEI.

My gratitude to Gail S. Taylor, D.Min., Richard O. Comfort, Th.D., Caroln Visser, M.Div., Barbara and Bill Owen, Shirley Bazar Steer, M.A., Kate deMedeiros, Ruth Braun, Elaine Hemenway, Sarah Wathen, Ann Fogelman, Greta Snow, Harriet Newman, Norma and Bob Shannon, and Sue and Don Wilkins who were participants in a Houston seminar. They helped in the selection of the book title and were invaluable in narrowing the field.

Cathy Schmermund, my editor, persevered through computer crashes and major tropical storms. I wish to thank Cathy for her dedication to the task. I am blessed to have had her considerable editing ability applied to the book.

My publisher, Brockton Brown, has the gift of encouragement. His even disposition and gentle spirit brought a special blessing to the process of publishing this book. I am very grateful for the opportunity to work with him.

I want to thank my children who formed a formidable cheering section during the process of bringing the book to completion. Judie Coutts, Marianne Isham, Lisa Macalaster, Brent Sullivan, Jamie Sullivan and my daughter-in-law Toni Sullivan have all been cheering me on.

Inspiration for the book has come from my grandchildren Julie Macalaster, Andrews Macalaster, Brent Sullivan, Sabrina Isham, Bryan Isham and my nieces Meredith Sabye, Lee Ward, Perrin Moriarty, Anna Moriarty, Caroline Moriarty and my nephews Charlie Ward, Joe Moriarty, Tommy Moriarty and Marty Sabye. It is my dearest wish that they will mature into spiritual elders and people of real worth.

Without the daily love and encouragement of my husband, Ivan Szuts, this book would not have been completed. It was interrupted by a cross-country move to Houston and, as soon as we were settled, it was Ivan who persuaded me to continue to work on the manuscript. He is a loving spirit and I am grateful for his unflagging support.

Never doubt that a small group of thoughtful, committed citizens can change the world. Indeed, it is the only thing that ever does.

Margaret Mead

Table of Contents

Introduction

In the early nineteen nineties, I was directing the Suffolk County Respite Care Program in New York, which provided much-needed relief for the caregivers of people with Alzheimer's disease. Part of my responsibility was to develop a training program for the volunteers — a dedicated group of elders in their fifties, sixties, seventies and even a few in their eighties.

As I reviewed the literature on aging, there was sufficient information available to develop training materials on its physical, emotional and intellectual aspects. However, I found there was a real void of material related to the spiritual level. During my search for spiritual material, I came upon the recently established work of Rabbi Zalman Schachter-Shalomi, who created the Spiritual Eldering Institute (SEI) in Philadelphia in nineteen eighty-eight. When I called to speak with him, he invited me to attend his one-week spiritual eldering program at Omega Institute in Rhinebeck, New York. The importance of his work was just beginning to be known when I went to study with him for the first time in the summer of 1993. During that special week, I experienced his profound insights into the spiritual aspects of aging. He was in the process of developing a training program for seminar leaders and I was later accepted into this program.

At the end of the Omega program, workshop participants were asked to think about how they might contribute to this emerging work. A group of us gathered together to brainstorm ideas and offer support. I immediately thought of developing a training curriculum for leaders who could turnkey this valuable work. As an educational administrator, I had worked with the development and dissemination of curricula for many years. So I volunteered to create the leader's curriculum. It was developed from Reb Zalman's manuscript of his landmark book, ***From Age-ing to Sage-ing: A Profound New Vision of Growing Older[1]***, my workshop lecture notes and suggestions from the eight original seminar leaders. As one of the first eight seminar leaders to be trained, I had the privilege of working closely with Reb Zalman, as he is known by his students. It was the beginning of a life-changing experience for me. Spiritual Eldering Institute seminars are currently being offered throughout the United States and Europe.

The vision for this book grew out of conversations with other seminar leaders and seminar participants. I began to become aware of the fact that, for the first time in human history, older women were asking questions that demanded answers: "What do I do with all these post-menopausal years in order to make my life meaningful?" "How can I use my increased healthspan to make a contribution to my planet?" In past generations, most women did not live long enough, after menopause, to ask such questions. Now there are ever-increasing numbers of us.

The popular opinion that views the elder years as a time for doing as one pleases, has had the effect of rendering senior citizens superfluous to society. With no —or limited—

expectations for ourselves, it is no wonder our society has come to see us as obsolete. We are free to choose obsolescence, but will it give meaning to our elder years?

I have discovered there are many among us who say, "No." We wish to prevent obsolescence, and see our challenge for the future as finding ways to remain vital. We prefer to define ourselves as elder women of worth, raising our self-respect and engendering respect from our larger society. It is my vision that together we'll create a planetary dialogue around common issues, generating a pragmatic "how to" manual for elder women of worth.

There is much needless suffering embedded in the western conception of aging for women. I am hoping that this book will open a dialogue around this needless suffering and help in diminishing it. A new consciousness, that supports our aging process, will be important for us and for future generations. To reveal the patterns in our society that repeat and harm will be an important task for she-elders. Collectively, we have the ability to create images of post-menopausal women as ***she-elder stateswomen***. If this book can serve as a catalyst for thoughtful transformation, into a higher consciousness about our aging process, then it will have been worth the writing.

She-Elder Stateswoman - a woman who will open physical and symbolic doors and encourage the emergence of she-elders in the third millennium. Like Maggie Kuhn, she will go right to the top to facilitate change.

Role clarification is an important task for women of worth as they discover the freedom to create who they will become is their elder years. Understanding the options opened to women in the past will help us to create our own version of the she-elder breaking through past stereotypes to be new women for a new millennium.

As we begin to adopt a "future-generations mentality" we will establish ourselves as future-oriented women. We can eliminate our own obsolescence and earn respect for what we are continuing to give to the planet.

With the sharing of my feelings, experiences, lessons learned and successes I invite other she-elders to share with me. This book expresses a feminine point of view and the profound changes that I have experienced through my participation in Spiritual Eldering Institute seminars, both as a student and as a seminar leader. It is my earnest desire to build on the work of Reb Zalman, stimulate further dialogue, and encourage a she-elder presence on the planet, as a positive force, in the third millennium.

This work fills a deep need, that I have, to find satisfaction in my elder years and to complete my life well. Not only do I wish to find a satisfying ending for my own personal life drama but I also desire to leave a special legacy for others and for the planet that has sustained me.

(1) Zalman Schachter-Shalomi. *From Age-ing to Sage-ing: A Profound New Vision of Growing Older.* New York: Warner Books, Inc., 1995.

I. Coming of Age

With a very different kind of woman coming of ripening age, in a world that is de-mythologized and culturally inter-connected there is, for the first time in all of world history, an opening for she-elders, in large numbers, to emerge. I find myself within this unique group of women and I hunger for a dialogue with other women facing this new reality. I am hopeful that the attuned mines among us will ignite she-elder energy and create the synergy that will bring elder woman-hood to a higher level of personal and collective experience. She-elders will no longer be invisible.

Who is the *she-elder*? A beginning description of a she-elder could be that she is consciously aware of all four levels of her being and she is oriented toward the future. She is conscious of her physical, emotional, intellectual and spiritual life. She is a woman, in a new millennium, with thirty to seventy-plus years to live after menopause, who will script the role of she-elder as she envisions it for herself. She is a new genre never before seen on this planet. She will come in a rainbow of colors. She will emerge from established religious traditions and secular organi-zations. A she-elder is a woman who will define herself as such, and in so doing, will change the planet. Both theorists and pragmatists will be needed to achieve the important worldwork in the first century of the third mil-lennium and beyond. The issues will be as varied as the women who pursue them. What will make the difference for the future is the raised consciousness of the group.

What will be my purpose as a she-elder? I have come to acknowledge the importance of consciously cultivating the ability to conserve my positive energy for well-defined objectives. It is also to cultivate the ability to recognize negative energy present in my life and work to transform that negative energy into something positive whenever possible. This transformed energy can then, with some thought, be placed into the human energy field in such a way as to positively impact both the present and the future of the planet.

The *emerging* she-elder will have the privilege of bringing to reality a fully-realized womanhood. A totally new breed of woman who walks the planet in the fullness of her body, mind, emotions and spirit. She will live consciously on all four levels of her experience. And our planet will never be the same.

Through personal revisioning each she-elder can construct her self-world. As we begin to value ourselves and think of ourselves as women of worth we are raising our collective value on the planet. Historically, the term elder came to mean one having authority by virtue of age and experience; an eminent senior member of a group or organization; or a person of earlier birth. The concept of dignity has often accompanied the term as well as the sense of an honorable life.

I think the term she-elder will enlarge the meaning of elder and the "she" will bring glorious gifts, as yet unopened, to the people of the planet. She-elders can use

their years between fifty and one hundred to do remark-
ably important things. They can address the future with
hope. She-elders can find meaningful roles for themselves
and their presence in society, in large numbers, will erase
the idea that seasoned women have no important roles to
play and are merely useless.

Ruth, a woman many years my senior, called me to say
that she had heard of the work that I was doing teaching
seminars for the Spiritual Eldering Institute. She told me
that she wanted desperately to be a part of something that
was future-oriented. Ruth who is a vital woman, in her late
seventies, finds herself surrounded with peers who spend their
days recounting their past. She told me that she did not wish
to spend her precious elder days recounting her social history and living in the past. She decided to focus her positive
energy on the future. There will be great numbers of she-
elders, like Ruth, emerging in the third millennium and the
planet will be she-elder enriched.

When she-elders begin to work in community with others who wish to be future-oriented then there will be a
significant impact. What does it mean to be in community?
To be in community has several meanings for me. My family
is a community, my church is a community, my neighbor-
hood is a community, my fellow seminar leaders at the
Spiritual Eldering Institute are a community and my worldwide internet correspondence is a community. An academic
friend of mine has a worldwide correspondence that she works
on each morning during her high-energy time. This energetic

eighty-seven year old she-elder does her world work at her desk in her study. I see myself using the internet as an invaluable tool for conserving energy and increasing worldwide communication throughout my elder years.

She-elders will create the *she-elder archetype*. This new model of seasoned womanhood will be identified and researched by future *herstorians*.

Contemporary she-elders will be the architects of this cosmic change that will ripple through the third millennium. This concept will need a lot of unpacking and I envision myself, along with other she-elders, making a contribution to this new archetype.

She-Elder Archetype - in process and may take a milleniumn to form.

Current she-elders, who have experienced glass ceilings in their work lives, as I and many others in my generation have, may give their energy to working on leveling the playing field for working women and help to create a meritocracy open to both men and women.

Other women like me, who were busy surviving in the work world during their middle years, may find great excitement in participating in the work of the spiritual eldering movement. Through personal revisioning each of us can create our elder world. When we talk of about the various levels in the world of work we use the metaphors of white collar, blue color, pink color and gold collar. In my mother's generation most of the women, who worked outside of the home wore pink collars. In my generation, impacted by the feminist movement, some of us struggled to move into white collar mid-management and above positions while many others remained in pink collars. My hope is that, symbolically speaking, all she-elders will wear gold collars demonstrating that they, as a group, are working on raising their collective value on the planet.

Gold-collar women, in large numbers, are a new phenomena. With a passionate purpose of our own creation we can enhance our self-esteem. Our new visibility, within the mainstream of our communities, will raise our collective value.

Contemporary she-elders may not have had the opportunity to participate in the feminist movement or the civil rights movement for a variety of valid reasons. But perhaps they will have the time, in their elder years, to embrace the spiritual eldering movement thereby helping to establish for themselves and future generations meaningful models for aging. The planet will become *she-elder enriched.*

The she-elder will work in community with others who also wish to be future-oriented. In community, these women of worth will customize their lifestyles. Some she-elders may choose to do worldwork. Some world

> **She-Elder Enriched** - the state of the planet when receiving the positive energy from women of worth.

work may require a physical presence outside of the home. Other worldwork, which we could call chairwork, could be accomplished from the home.

She-elders will help to create the she-elder archetype. Contemporary she-elders will be the architects of this cosmic change that will ripple through the third millennium. This concept will also need a lot of unpacking and I look forward to those dialogues.

The she-elder will reject the term gerontology (the study of old men) and find a neologism for the emerging body of literature about mature, attuned women. She will help to create new words for a new time. Perhaps the study of old women might be given its own name. It could be called *sherontology,* or some other "ology," giving us the recognition that we deserve. As a professor, teaching a variety of gerontology courses, I am concerned that the word gerontology is another example of the dominance of men in our society, even old men.

Do we want mature women to languish at the fringes of society with nothing meaningful to do? Most women of worth will reject obsolescence and will use their energy to impact an issue or issues of importance to them. To conceptualize oneself as a *Spiritual Elder, a Woman of Worth*, is to embrace significance. It is to see oneself as having an important role. It is a role that is not limiting and constraining but one of your own creation.

Herstory - the documentation of the work of women of all ages in the last century of the second millennium and the first century of the third millennium.

What will this moment in history, this new millennium, ask of me as a she-elder? This is a question that I must answer for myself. I would like to do it in community with other she-elders. Collectively, she-elders can write the lessons of future *herstory*.

Our introduction of a broadened vision of she-elderhood will be inspired by the sunrise-effect of the new millennium. It will color our work and we will know that we exist for such a time as

Herstorical Period - formed in the last century of the second millennium and gaining momentum in the first century of the third millennium.

this. This new *"herstorical period"* will be cross-cultural and inclusive. World womanhood will, in the process, redefine itself.

She-elder valuation is a concept that also needs unpacking. This concept insists that she-elders have a significant role to play in society. As she-elders design and assume these significant roles they will evolve as cultural centerpieces. These seasoned women, who have turned a corner on reality, will expose the cultural conspiracy to find reality in a certain way. They will change

She-Elder Valuation - a concept needing definition in the third millennium.

the reality of our society by first valuing themselves and then, collectively, valuing each other.

The dysfunctional mythologies, that have colored our world, will disappear under the watchful eyes of women of worth. Any feelings of uselessness will be replaced by usefulness. The planet will be blessed with the she-eldering presence.

Many women, like myself, have made choices, within historical and cultural contexts, that may have been limiting for them. Emerging she-elders may have experienced expanded opportunity as a result of the women's movement. This expansion of choices, open to us, has also caused some division among us. In order to put understanding into our she-elder relationships we need to honor and accept each others' life choices by saying to each other "how deeply I respect the choices you have made." Indeed, future generations of she-elders may not want what current generations have wanted. They will establish their own agendas and that is how it should be.

Contemporary she-elders can help to diffuse the fogginess on the road ahead. One of their important tasks will be to create new roles in large numbers, embody these roles and refine them. They will mid-wife this new, ripening, feminine archetype for future generations.

The she-elders are coming and will create a plethora of positions and purpose for both he-elders and she-elders. Job creation will be a major goal for some women of worth. Wisdom work could be another goal. World work still another. Inner spiritual eldering work will be prerequisite for all as it will allow the fully-realized she-elder to emerge.

Future portrait artists will place on canvas the new image of she-elders. When future generations ask, "What is the visage of a she-elder?," they will see many examples. And they will all be significant.

With still so much to give and the willingness to give to the world, can we spiritual elders, conscious of the importance of our mission, find a way to empower others in our world community? It will be a process, and may take a quarter century to accomplish but, at this time of life, many of us have the gift of time. We emerging she-elders are approaching a millennium that will change humanity in significant ways. We can play an important part in creating the roles, images and impact of she-elders.

In the following chapters we will look at the spirit, mind,

body and emotions of she-elders. We will also explore some research on the roles of older women and some lifestyle choices. The world of the mature woman is increasingly a society of elder women. As we spend some time looking at the roles and lifestyle choices of mature women we will be energized by the opportunities and excited by the meaningful realities that can be achieved.

Will she-elders spend their time ignoring or patching up the old world view? They can do that or they can choose to make a "mind move." As part of the earth's brain cells they can help to create a dramatic shift. This shift to creating meaningful she-elderhoods is only beginning.

Margaret Mead thought that if our society is to survive we would have to empower each other through citizens' volunteer associations and ongoing teaching-learning communities. Saging centers are currently being developed. These centers would bring together elders for personal and world work.

If we are currently threatened by the non-equilibrium dynamics of the large numbers of she-elders on the horizon then we can be equally challenged by their awesome presence and potential power. The early cohorts of she-elders may have to content themselves with the idea that they may not live to see all the important work accomplished but they will have made a start.

Over the past few years it has become clear to me that this moment in history is asking something enormous of women and that, which is being asked will take form in the early decades of the third millennium as an educated, socially-conscious and often privileged womanhood approaches she-elderhood.

The era, in world history, that responded to Plato, Aristotle, Buddha, Isaiah, Jeremiah, Confuscious and Zarathustra created an integration of the male global brain and moved the male human experience to new heights. Something similar has happened in the last fifty years of the second millennium. We have witnessed the empowerment of large numbers of women on the spiritual, physical, intellectual and emotional levels. The emergence of women of great thought and action, in disciplines associated with the quadrinity, has empowered the women's movement. It has created a new phenomenon. It has readied the world for the integration of the female global brain. Margaret Mead, Jean Houston, Leah Rabin, Ruth Jacobs, Mother Teresa, Golda Meir, Coretta Scott King, Madeline Albright, Gloria Steinem, Betty Freidan, Gay Luce, Maya Angelou and many, many other contemporary artists, writers and scholars are contributing to the she-elder brain evolution.

The universal women's movement is fortunate to have had extraordinary leadership in the twentieth century. These women of courage and intellect broke the ideological trail with their vision for future women of worth. These pioneers, of historical note, were often singular figures crying in the wilderness. In contrast, she-elders of the third millennium will be great in number.

The social infrastructure that will be constructed for

seasoned women will outdistance anything ever conceived of in all of world history. We can work to create a social safety net in which all women of any color, sexual persuasion, or lifestyle choice will be protected throughout their lives. While encouraging the self-scripting of women's lives, she-elders will create a universal template for security within which she-elders will be protected from the vagaries of long life. To increase satisfaction and lessen fear in long life will be a major goal of the emerging spiritual she-elder movement.

The women, who choose to resonate to these ideas, will take a piece of the worldwork and create the mission that they will fulfill by themselves or with a community of other women of worth. She-elders will want their long lives to count. They now have the opportunity, for the first time in history, to improve the world for themselves and for other long-lived she-elders.

Questions To Ponder About Our Evolving She-Elders.

1. Why is this time in history uniquely different for she-elders?

2. Who is a she-elder?

3. What kind of she-elder work will I do for the planet?

4. What she-elder work needs to be done collectively with other she-elders?

5. What is my concept of my ideal woman of worth?

6. How does the excitement of living into a new age impact my thinking?

7. What kind of "new think" will empower my mind?

8. How can I honor and accept the life choices of other she-elders?

9. How can I keep on evolving into she-elderhood?

10. Will I be focused on the past, future or both?

2. Body

My grandaunt Mae was a faded beauty in her sixties, when I was a little girl. I remember her porcelain skin, mostly unlined. I also remember her dyed black hair that seemed inconsistent with her age even to me as a child. My father told me that she had lied about her age, all of her adult life, so that when it came time for her to collect social security, she had quite a problem proving that she was, indeed, sixty-five years old. Apparently, the trail of incorrect records she had created over her working life had come back to haunt her. As I think about it now, I realize that as a single working woman, she may have felt the need to protect herself from both ageism and sexism in a male-dominated work world.

Aunt Mae

On the other hand, my grandaunt Kathryn, Mae's sister, a member of the same cohort group, aged very differently. She, too, was a single working woman of the same era. She "went to business" and supported herself throughout her adult life. I remember her as being very comfortable in her mature body. She had lovely, soft hair that framed her face. It was blue-rinsed as was the custom at that time. She had a regalness and a dignity befitting her years. She was a lovely addition to all our family gatherings. I remember her as having aged very gracefully.

Aunt Kathryn

As our bodies age are we of less value to the community? Has our communal net worth diminished? Will we continue to feel the need to lie about our aging bodies in the third millennium? Or will we own our ages and bodies at each stage we enter? How will women of worth deal with physical aging?

Body Language

As I made my way into my middle fifties, the word "over-qualified" became a standard reply as I sought upper management positions. I was in excellent health and my attendance records were outstanding. But somehow, I had slipped into a category called "overqualified." Several friends told me to interpret the word "overqualified" as meaning I was too old for the position. But what did "too old" mean? Did it mean I would bring less energy to the job? Definitely not. I had learned to conserve my energy and use it in the most beneficial ways. I no longer squandered my energy on trivial pursuits. My body had not let me down. It was supporting my daily activities more efficiently than ever.

So what had changed? The world's perception of me had changed. That perception was a leftover from an earlier era. I resented the limitations this communal perception put on me. I want it to change, and it will, by large numbers of us demonstrating our capabilities. But how will we find those opportunities? There is work to be done here. We need to erase the old perception that the body becomes incapable at a certain age. Women of worth, who have made wellness their standard operating system, can change this perception. This may take a generation or two to change, but it is possible.

Honoring Our Aging Bodies

One of the ways Reb Zalman taught me to honor my body is by owning its age. Now, when asked about my age, I respond in terms of my "years of life experience," always giving the correct number at the moment. There were some middle years of my life when I was tempted not to tell my age when asked. That doesn't happen any more.

Reb Zalman

People often tell my friend Judith that she doesn't look her age. She just smiles and responds, "Yes I do. This is what fifty-nine is supposed to look like for me." Is she helping to change a misconception about aging bodies? You bet she is, and we are blessed to have *perception pioneering* women like Judith.

By being in our mature bodies and treating those bodies with the respect they deserve, we will model positive women of worth body language. These vessels have served us faithfully through the years, bringing us all the way to our post-menopausal years. By respecting our bodies, we will radiate this message and receive the courtesy and respect from the young that we gave to our elders. When we are ready to receive this courtesy, we will send out body language that invites a courteous response.

While attending a Conscious Aging Conference several years ago, I was privileged to share a room with a very special woman. Florence, from Florida, had seventy years of life

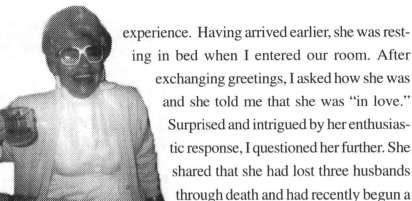

Florence
Ross

experience. Having arrived earlier, she was rest-
ing in bed when I entered our room. After
exchanging greetings, I asked how she was
and she told me that she was "in love."
Surprised and intrigued by her enthusias-
tic response, I questioned her further. She
shared that she had lost three husbands
through death and had recently begun a
relationship with another gentleman. She
was deeply in love with him and it showed. Even though she
had loved and lost three times, she was still willing to love
again. Her giving spirit and love of life radiated from her body.

Later, when she arose to shower and dress, she did so
completely naked. She walked with such self-assurance and
dignity that I was overwhelmed. She was completely at ease
in her seventy-year-old body and made no negative comments
about it during the entire weekend we were roommates. It
was obvious that she enjoyed and appreciated her body. She
was at home in it.

I am trying very hard to become comfortable with my
maturing body. To be as comfortable as Florence is, will
be a real stretch for me. But I'm working on it. I'm very
grateful for women like Florence, who inspire those of us
who are younger.

Being Responsible For Our Bodies

Taking personal responsibility for our own bodies and
their proper functioning is a concept that has begun to be

more widely recognized. During the May 1995 White House Conference on Aging, for example, number ten of the forty-five resolutions adopted as the national aging agenda for the next decade addressed this issue. The defining statements of this resolution include the following:

(1) Whereas, individuals make choices about the food that they eat, the physical activity/exercise in which they engage and the life-style they lead;

(2) Whereas, many health problems can be prevented or alleviated by changes in behavior, lifestyle, or treatment plan;

(3) Whereas, all individuals, including older individuals and their families and caregivers, need adequate information to make informed choices about health care, personal assistance, and rehabilitation services;

(4) Whereas, well informed health care providers and recipients create more efficient and effective health care services;

(5) Whereas, cultural differences influence and determine life-style choices and opportunities;

(6) Whereas, older adults are normally their own primary providers of health care;

Therefore, be it resolved by the 1995 White House Conference on Aging to support policies that:

* Ensure that all individuals, especially older adults and caregivers, have full access to wellness and health educational programs, services, and facilities so they may provide sufficient self care and know when to seek appropriate professional care.

1. **Invest time** to think about your lifestyle
2. **Invest time** to examine your health problems
3. **Invest time** to think about your health care information sources
4. **Invest time** to think about the effectiveness of your health care services.
5. **Invest time** to think about the impact of your culture on your lifestyle.
6. **Invest time** to think about the ways you provide health care to yourself on all four levels.

* Provide information to all persons, especially older adults, about disease prevention, and detection; chronic disease management; accident prevention; the consequences of smoking, substance abuse, and poor nutrition; emergency response technology, mental health and wellness programs.
* Educate all persons in the community about the diversity of the aging process, including possible physical, emotional and social changes affecting older adults, and evaluate the effectiveness of such educational programs.
* Utilize and promote traditional and non-traditional means as well as new technologies and innovative approaches to distribute information to older adults, their families and caregivers, including the frail elderly and individuals who are homebound or institutionalized, and include follow up support.
* Ensure that approaches and materials are culturally and linguistically appropriate and accessible to both urban and rural populations.
* Implement/expand the Indian Health Service Elder Health Program to provide geriatric/gerontological training and elder wellness programs, and require that all programs of the Indian Health Service, including tribal and urban health programs, have access to prevention, promotion, and wellness programs.[1]

What will women of worth bring to these issues? Our national agenda may be an inspiration for us to use our skills, in a paid or volunteer capacity, to address these challenges.

"I came to that place where I woke up. It made me take responsibility for who I will become tomorrow," says Reb Zalman. Where will we wake up? Who will we be tomorrow? We can take responsibility for our bodies and be grateful for their life-sustaining work. We can reject the cultural images that are thrust on us and get in touch with our own bodies. We can work toward the consciousness needed to have the longest possible healthspan and the shortest possible disability span. By so doing, we'll use less of our scarce medical resources and be perceived by future generations as an asset, not a liability, to society.

Touch

How can we raise our consciousness about our bodies? One way is through massage. It literally puts us in touch with ourselves and helps us learn how to take care of ourselves.

While massaging my hands recently, for example, I noticed the beginning of an arthritic joint in the little finger of my left hand. Since I'm left-handed and really enjoy good penmanship and writing in my journal, this discovery was very alarming. But once aware of this bodily change, I could take action. I bought a squeezable ball that I keep in my car and use when I wait at red lights. I also started taking a gelatine-juice drink just before bedtime. Since osteoarthritis is in my genes, I may not be able to prevent it from developing in my body. But with proper nutrition and exercise, I can delay its onset and increase my healthspan.

I have begun to journal about how it feels when I touch each body part and what that body part has meant to me over the years. Making my hands available to touch myself lovingly has been a gift I have bestowed upon myself. It is also a "priceless" gift that we can give to others that doesn't cost anything but time. Jesus, a master-teacher, demonstrated his servanthood by washing his disciples' feet. As we age, we may have a tendency to brag about what we have accomplished in life. Massaging another person's feet could be excellent humility training, and a much-needed gift of touch for another.

photo by Lisa Sullivan

Hugs

A hug is another great gift. One size fits all and it's easy to exchange. Double hugs are twice as good as single hugs. You give the first hug by opening your arms as far as you can and raising one arm and lowering the other. Then you step back, raise and lower the opposite arms and give a second hug. This is so much fun and it doubles the pleasure of greeting friends and family.

When I was in college, I had to write a term paper on my perception of my parents' relationship. I was asked to determine what I thought was good and bad about it and then draw some conclusions for my own life. After completing the assignment, I sat reading it with tears streaming down my cheeks. I realized that I had never seen my parents hug or kiss each other. And although I felt loved by my parents, they seldom showed it by holding, hugging or kissing me. The conclusion that I drew from this was that my own family would be a "huggy-kissy" family. And we are. We would not dream of arriving or departing without hugging each other. My son, who is shy about his feelings, gives me great big bear hugs, which I treasure.

Jamie, Brent and Lisa 1981

When we encounter an elder with arthritis, however, we have to be conscious about giving gentle hugs, so we don't cause discomfort. Hopefully, I will never get so arthritic that I will not want to be hugged.

Healers

I've had personal experience with the healing power of touch. While at the Spiritual Eldering Workshop in the summer of 1995, I was stung by a bee. Since I am not allergic to bee stings, I continued my dyadic work with another participant. At the break, I told the workshop leader, Bahira, that I would return after going to the nurse for some pain reliever. Bahira asked if she could do a Reiki healing on me. When I agreed, she took my arm and placed her hand above the sting, which was radiating much heat. We stood quietly together for several minutes while she moved her hand above the reddened area. After less than ten minutes, she

Reiki healing: REI (ray) means universal life energy, spiritual consciousness and all-knowing. KI (kee) means breathe, lifeforce and vital energy.

removed her hand and the redness, heat and pain were gone. To have been touched and healed by one of my peers is a powerful experience. The value of such healers will become more recognized as more women develop these skills.

There are also holistic physicians, like Chrisitana Northrup, whose practice in Maine is dedicated to women's health. She speaks at many conferences in an effort to inspire women to detoxify their bodies and be responsible for them. She is one of many healers changing the face of women's medicine.

It is a time to heal? How can we heal? We can think about what we can personally do to promote wellness. I recently started a wellness business with the dream of bringing comfort to others. I became a distributor for a company that makes products designed to increase energy and personal comfort. It is what I can do now to promote my own wellness, and that of my friends, relatives and anyone with whom I come in contact. In my early professional years, I taught nutrition to teenagers. Now, in my later years, I wish to learn and teach wellness to my peers. It is a time to heal.

Sacred Sexuality

Our post-menopausal years can be a time to explore sacred sexuality or High Sex. In her book entitled *The Art of Sexual Ecstasy: The Path of Sacred Sexuality for Western Lovers*, Margo Anand focuses on love and ecstasy training taking a look at our sexual energy from the "sacred" or "tantric" perspective could give us new insight into the use of this energy. She shares the following insight:

Connecting with a partner in High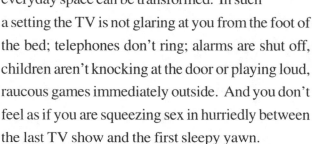
Sex requires a special haven that is
dedicated to lovemaking as a form of art.
If you have a place that can be set aside for
that purpose, wonderful. If you do not, an
everyday space can be transformed. In such
a setting the TV is not glaring at you from the foot of
the bed; telephones don't ring; alarms are shut off,
children aren't knocking at the door or playing loud,
raucous games immediately outside. And you don't
feel as if you are squeezing sex in hurriedly between
the last TV show and the first sleepy yawn.

This sanctuary should not only afford protection
from the outside world, but positively contribute to
extraordinary lovemaking. It should be your Persian
garden of pleasure, your Tantric temple of sexual
fulfillment, your Japanese teahouse of ultimate
delight. This is your Sacred Space, a place designed
to create the conditions for ecstatic lovemaking. It
is an environment for bliss.[2]

The first fundamental of High Sex, that Anand teaches,
is that the source of sexual pleasure is within you and does
not depend on connecting with an ideal partner. Anand em-
phasizes that it is not necessary to have a partner to achieve
high sex. Women without partners may be grateful for this
knowledge.

She stresses the importance of developing imagination
for enhancing intimacy. She tells us that, 'It is the ability to

create is your mind's eye a vision of what is possible so that you can mobilize your talents to actualize it."[3]

Imagination is not the *same* as fantasy. Fantasizing is pretending that something is happening that you don't expect could ever happen, whereas imagination enables you to act as if something were actually true. For example, it is pure fantasy to expect that you will win the lottery and thereby solve all your financial problems. But imagining the fulfillment of your sexual potential is well within your grasp. Imagination reveals not only limits that prevent us from changing and growing but also ways to explore and transcend them. It bridges the gap between what we are and what we may be.[4]

There will be many more of us living healthy, sexually-active lives and there will be more research in this area in the future. Part of our responsibility may be to participate in this research and build the body of literature around sexual issues of concern to she-elders, We can also help to dismantle the myths about elder sexuality like the one that says elders no longer have any interest in sex.

Since the endocrine system and the brain control our sexuality how we think about it may have a powerful effect on our sexual enjoyment. One of the gifts of elderhood is having time to think and to explore new ways of bringing joy into our lives.

Body Talk

Feminist writer Barbara MacDonald points out that a large proportion of women's conversations—at any age—are about our bodies. Adolescent girls compare notes about breast development and menstrual periods. Young women discuss breast implants, contraception and pregnancy. Later in life, we address pre-menopausal, peri-menopausal and post-menopausal issues, hysterectomies and mastectomies, thanks to the feminist generation that brought these interests out into the open.

Best-sellers, such as ***Ourselves Growing Older***, by the Boston Women's Health Book Collective and ***The Silent Passage*** by Gail Sheehy have helped give a voice to these mature body interests. Women of worth can continue to promote forums where discussions about mature female body issues and end-of-life body issues can take place.

Inquiry Into Life Extension

This longer healthspan should be an exciting time. Our bodies may demand more care and time, but many of us will have more time to provide that care. Carl Jung said:

> A human being would certainly not grow to be seventy or eighty years old if this longevity had no meaning for the species. The afternoon of human life must also have a significance of its own and cannot be merely a pitiful appendage to life's morning. Whoever carries over into the afternoon the law of the morning must pay for it with damage to his soul.

Both of my grandmothers passed before their fiftieth birthdays. I ask myself why am I still alive? Finding the answer to that question will be essential to being a spiritual-elder, woman of worth.

Speaking Up

Speaking in public, in a proactive way, about the major issues before women is a gift given only to a few. But speaking privately, raising the consciousness of one other, is the privilege of all women. In the next millennium, women of worth will raise their voices privately and collectively. The voices may even take on "intergenerational harmony" over the next few decades, with four and five generations of women recognizing their interdependence. I look forward to working on women's health issues to enlighten my elderhood and that of future generations.

The Inner Body

Each morning, I have an opportunity to consciously assess my body and be grateful for all the parts that are working well. Looking upon my body in this positive way is a blessing.

I also have the opportunity to consciously pay attention to the messages that my body sends to me. If I am receiving pain signals, I have a responsibility to look for the cause — not just mask it with painkillers. If the cause is lifestyle-related, then I know I'll have to examine my life choices and establish a program that will effect the necessary change. If some functional losses begin to accompany the maturing process, I can decide to compensate for these changes rather than complain about them. The compensation may take the form of a regimen that I follow. This program begins in my mind.

When I became peri-menopausal, for example, I chose to start Hormone Replacement Therapy (HRT). It's a choice that's new to my generation and comes with risks and advantages. Many women choose not to do this therapy for good reasons. It will take extensive research to learn the answers to the questions that we are asking. And we may not live long enough to get those answers. However, I believe that I am doing something good for my body and that belief sustains me.

Each morning and evening, when I take my vitamin supplements, I perform a sacred ceremony. As I place each nutritional supplement in my mouth, I bless my body for continued good health. The consciousness with which I perform this ceremony has turned simple pill taking into a ritual for my well being.

The nourishment we select for our bodies will become our future selves. As women of worth, we realize that our tomorrow depends on today's choices. I have to continue to tell myself that if I desire a healthy future, I must be responsible today.

One of the advantages of becoming a woman of worth is recognizing the causes of negative reactions that occur within our physical beings. Over the years, I have enjoyed chocolate in a variety of forms. It took many years before I realized that each time I chose to eat chocolate, I experienced a skin reaction within twenty-four hours. I finally decided to eliminate chocolate from my diet. By forcing my body to accept a food that triggered a negative response, I was placing unnecessary strain on it. I may still be severely tempted when I'm offered chocolate, until I remind myself that if I want a healthy future, I'd better be responsible today.

Taking responsibility for what we can control about our bodies requires being totally conscious of our daily living. One simple way of being aware of what we take into our bodies is to pause before eating. I learned to do this from my friend Steffi. Placing her hands on either side of her plate, she takes a few moments to look at the nourishment before her and to be grateful for it. If we see sustenance on our plates that we deem to be good for us, we will send positive messages to our brains.

Plastic Fantastic?

At a Spiritual Eldering workshop, one of the participants concluded after scanning the room that there were at least two participants in the group who had had facelifts. She asked if I could pick them out. Since true to the Institute's emphasis on owning our ages, we had already heard each person reveal their real age. It was easy to identify the women with facelifts. I remember thinking, at the time, how silly these women were to be in denial of aging. Since then, however, I have pondered the reasons mature women may choose cosmetic surgery for their bodies. I concluded that there are many valid reasons and that women should be supported in those decisions.

My friend Elizabeth purchased a wonderful portrait of a long-lived woman and brought it to our sharing meeting. Steffi and I were struck by the beauty and magnificence of the character lines in the woman's face. The same week, Elizabeth took the picture to another women's group and found a far different response. These women commented about the deep lines in the woman's face and suggested that a facelift would be necessary to improve her appearance.

The changing consciousness about "beauty" must leave room for both of these expressions. While there may always be a place for cosmetic surgery, perhaps with increasing value as women of worth in society, more of us will wear our character lines with pride and dignity.

My friend Sarah recently had a facelift. What changed for Sarah, following her surgery, was not so much her appearance, but how she felt about herself. She glowed with excitement, and I was happy for her because she now liked herself. I appreciated her openness in discussing her surgery with me. I often wonder why so many women try to keep their surgeries a secret. We may know the answer to this question in the future as more women choose cosmetic surgery. I now live in one of the plastic surgery capitals of the world—Houston, Texas—and I am bombarded with advertisements every day. I examine the marketing behind the ads and wonder if this is yet another male exploitation of women like the hysterectomy hysteria of my mother's generation.

Or is it something of true worth to women?

I have many questions about cosmetic surgery. I can get the intellectual answers to my questions by going to web sites like the American Society of Plastic and Reconstructive Surgeons, and review the cases and procedures by different doctors. But how do women respond emotionally and physically to cosmetic changes? I look forward to a dialogue about this with other women of worth in the next millennium.

Cosmetics On The Body

The addition of color to the face and other body parts has long been a cross-cultural tradition. While watching a video on the Woman's Spirituality movement, I was struck by the beautiful cosmetic artistry women applied to their faces as they prepared for a ritual ceremony. I began to wonder why many of us choose to place color on our faces and make it a daily ritual. We can and do welcome the addition of color to our lives. Why do we put color on our face?

However, many women choose not to wear any color on their faces and, instead, rely on their natural hues to express their inner beauty. Some of the loveliest faces I have ever seen have been nuns who don't wear any makeup. Their inner beauty shines through.

The important point here is to raise our consciousness about the choices that we make. If we do choose to put makeup on our faces, could that become a ritual? If makeup were to become an appropriate ritual, how could we make that time more meaningful?

Cleansing Ceremonies

In a camp washroom one summer, I watched a mature woman cup her hands and lovingly rinse her face with clear water. That experience left a lasting impression on me. Her ritual of bathing suggested a sacredness that I had never before experienced. It raised my consciousness about caring for the spirit while cleansing the body. The conscious motion of her hands as she gently brought clear water to her face told me that she had thought about this cleansing ceremony and that it was important to her.

Sheriatrics

If Asclepiades of Bethynia is the father of geriatrics who, might we ask, is the *"mother of sheriatrics?"* It's only in the very last years of the twentieth century that women's medicine and physical problems have received attention. Female physicians and researchers are creating a new archetype for future generations of women to look up to and emulate. As a young person, I never knew a female physician. Now I am delighted to know female physicians both professionally and personally.

Will there be a female physician, in the next millennium, who will arise to lead the women's health movement? Will she insist on equal research money and equal media time for women's health issues? As large numbers of us age, we will be looking for just such a leader.

Mother of Sheriatrics - a woman, who will rise to global prominence, and place post-menopausal women's medical issues on the world agenda.

Christiane Northrup, M.D., founder of "Women to Women," a women-treating-women health clinic in Yarmouth,

Maine is a visionary in women's health and wellness. She is one of the leaders in women's medicine, who is helping shift us to a new paradigm in health care.

In her book ***Women's Bodies Women's Wisdom: Creating Physical and Emotional Health and Healing*** she states the following insight:

> We have been taught that our disease-care system is supposed to keep us healthy. We have been socialized to turn to doctors whenever we have concerns about our bodies and our health. We have been taught the myth of the medical gods — that doctors know more than we do about our bodies, that the expert holds the cure. It's no wonder that when I ask women to tell me what's going on in their bodies, they sometimes reply, 'You tell me; you're the doctor!' Doctors are authority figures for some women, right up there with their husbands and priests. Yet, each woman is more knowledgeable about herself than anyone else."[5]

Caroline Myss, Ph.D. tells us in ***Why People Don't Heal and How They Can*** that:

> In any event, the image of allopathic medicine as the enemy is no longer valid or useful. After initially resisting alternative healing modalities, the medical establishment in recent years has opened itself to a number of non-traditional methods: reflexology,

chiropractic, massage and acupuncture; the use of vitamins, enzymes, amino acids and other vital supplements; and the use of nutritional treatments to combat free radicals, the elements in the body that support the development of illness. The advantage to recognizing both traditional and allopathic medical possibilities is there's a much wider range of healing energy from which to choose.[6]

Northrup and Myss have given us wisdom to live by and great hope for a healthy future.

(1) "Official 1995 White House Conference on Aging Adopted Resolutions." Washington, D.C., May 1995. pg. 6-7.
(2) Margo Anand, *The Art of Sexual Ecstasy—The Path of Sacred Sexuality for Western Lovers.* G.P.Putnam's Sons, New York, 1997. pg. 68.
(3) ibid., pg. 105.
(4) ibid., pg. 106.
(5) Christiane Northrup, M.D., *Women's Bodies, Women's Wisdom: Creating Physical and Emotional Health and Healing.* New York: Bantam Books. 1994. pg. 9.
(6) Caroline Myss, Ph.D., *Why People Don't Heal and How They Can.* New York: Harmony Books. 1997. pg. 144-145.

Questions To Ponder About
Our Bodies.

1. How honest am I about my physical age?

2. How does my attitude about my physical age effect my life?

3. How could the way I talk about my physical body effect the attitudes future generations have about their bodies?

4. How can I respect the choices of other women?

5. How do I care for my aging body?

6. Why am I alive today?

7. How am I incorporating wellness practices into my life in order to increase my healthspan?

8. What role do cosmetics play in my life?

9. How do I feel about cosmetic surgery?

10. How do I bring bodily discomfort upon myself?

11. How important is touching and being touched in my life?

12. What morning and evening rituals could I establish to support a healthy body?

3. Mind

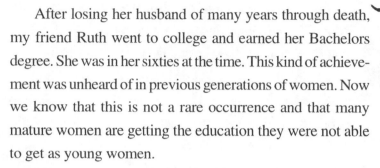

After losing her husband of many years through death, my friend Ruth went to college and earned her Bachelors degree. She was in her sixties at the time. This kind of achievement was unheard of in previous generations of women. Now we know that this is not a rare occurrence and that many mature women are getting the education they were not able to get as young women.

What do women like Ruth hope to achieve with their degrees? They tell me that they wish to improve the quality of their own minds. They want to keep their minds in an expanding mode and make a contribution to the world with their new learning. One energetic woman of worth named Vivian is working on a Doctorate in mediation. Vivian is in her early seventies. Her dream is to accompany a significant leader on a world peace mission. She wishes to bring a measure of peace to a troubled world. Do you think that the world needs wise women as mediators? Think of the women of great intellect who have arrived on the world stage as heads of state and diplomats. Their impact has been significant. For the first time in history women's issues are at the top of some diplomatic agendas.

As women of worth grow older, they become less and less alike. The research tells us that we differentiate. The uniqueness of each she-elder mind, with a perspective on life that has been fine-tuned over five-plus decades, becomes a resource of inestimable worth. As we age, our minds can explore, with a longer view, the impact of the influences that have formed it.

Photo by Sara Barrett

Gail Sheehy

Gail Sheehy's ***New Passages: Mapping Your Life Across Time*** tells us that the combined effects of genes, gender, race, class, marital status, income and preventive healthcare all begin to add up. Our health status and longevity are largely genetically determined, until we reach age sixty or sixty-five. After that, if we have escaped catastrophic illness during the critical middle life period — from forty-five to sixty-five — it is our psychological attitude and behavior that are most likely to determine the quality and duration of our later years.[1]

If it is our mindset that will determine the quality of our third age, then it becomes extremely important to take a look at our attitudes toward ourselves, our families and the world. We might do some journaling about questions like, "What do I think about myself as a woman of worth?" As we begin to answer these questions, we move toward clarity of mind.

Shentellect - the critical mass of intellectual capital created by mature, educated women of worth.

With all our minds, coalescing in the third millennium, women of worth could make the quintessential difference on our planet. This group intelligence, if focused, could move us to a higher level of existence. This synergistic intellectual energy has begun to manifest itself in the last quarter of the twentieth century and could reach significant impact in the first decade of the twenty-first century. Boosting the collective intelligence of the planet is a major challenge for women of worth. I have come to think of this intellectual capital as ***shentellect.***

A Whack On The Head

While attending a Conscious Aging Conference I told another participant, about the Barbara Walker book, *The Crone: Woman of Age, Wisdom, and Power*, that I had read recently. I explained how the book had opened my mind to some new thinking. My friend turned to me and stated that I had gotten "a whack on the head."

Opening the mind to new thinking, as a woman of worth, requires work. It's much easier to stay with "old think;" it's comfortable and requires no courage. But keeping an open mind is essential for conscious and effective intellectual work. A symbolic "whack on the head" opened my mind and one of my main goals as a woman of worth is to keep it open. I needed that whack on the head, that wake-up call. I continue to be very grateful for it.

In retrospect, I know that getting the figurative whack on the head awakened my sensitivity to old archetypes. It inspired me to search for new and more relevant ones. Perhaps, the time has come to create a totally new archetype that will inspire future generations of women of worth. Have the male and female archetypes, known throughout history, moved us closer to becoming fully conscious humans? Perhaps, but I believe the time has come for the "woman-of-worth archetype" that includes the mind, body, emotions and spirit of elder women, to emerge.

While studying to become a Spiritual Eldering Institute seminar leader, I was preparing a lesson on archetypes. In reviewing the feminine archetypes, I realized that none of them embodied the completeness of the third-millennium woman I envision. A part of me could identify with each of them, but at the same time, each archetype represented only a facet of what I wish to become. I knew that as a third-millennium woman of worth, I represented a new breed of woman with a rich opportunity to continue to expand my brain power. I also knew that I would grow into my elder years differently from the generations of women that preceded me. And I knew that there would be many other pioneers like me.

I began to think of this conscious and expanded feminine *shentellect* and to consider what it could contribute to the betterment of the planet. Maybe a whack on the side of the head is necessary to motivate us to dismantle any dysfunctional mythologies that need to be eliminated for the future. When any woman of worth slips into thinking that her intellectual accomplishments are behind her, she needs to think again. Maybe she could use a "whack on the head," too.

Interpreting Shentellect

If future artists can find a way to express this critical mass of intellectual capital created by mature, educated women of worth perhaps we'll have new figures to view. Public buildings, parks and educational structures could be adorned with sculpture and works of art that embody women of worth archetypes with seasoned minds. Women of worth could develop powerful new images, for future world societies, to uplift and engage their minds. When we begin to accept the idea that our best thinking is still in our future then we can avoid stagnation and keep our minds open.

New Think

Am I listening to myself talking? I have developed thought and speech patterns that have been a part of my repertoire for years. As a woman of worth, I am learning to listen to myself talk. I am consciously aware of what I am saying. I ask myself the following questions: Are these the same old lines that I have been expressing for years? Are these the same old thoughts that I have been thinking for years? If the answer is yes, then I have to consciously examine my thinking to see if it's *frontier thinking.* Or does my thinking reflect a social-historical period with little relevance to the future?

Margaret Kemeny, a research psychologist at UCLA, predicts that we are on the frontier of understanding how psychological changes relate to very specific changes in physiology. Her study shows that being happy or depressed even for twenty minutes, affects the number and activity of natural "good" killer cells in the bloodstream.[2] The impact of our thinking on our emotions, and that impact on our bodies, will be key to being fulfilled women of worth.

Gail Sheehy tells us that people with positive outlooks, who continue to connect themselves to the future and marshal their energies to defeat depression or entropy, are far more likely to extend their second adulthood into healthy and satisfying lives. But we have to reach for it. It doesn't come to us. We need a new ambition. We need to make life happen for us. The decision to renew ourselves requires a real investment of faith, risk and physical discipline. [3]

Happy Endings

Andrew Greeley, the Roman Catholic priest who writes romantic novels, defined a romantic as someone who believes in happy endings. I am a romantic and I believe in happy endings. I believe that I can create my own happy ending in my mind. If I cannot believe in this possibility, then how can I expect my life to end well? How can I expect it to end happily?

The first time that I went to the Spiritual Eldering Institute at Omega I participated in a role-playing session of a death-bed scenario with Sarah, a woman in her late seventies. I sat on the grass, in the lovely herb garden, with Sarah's head cradled in my lap. She was stretched out on the lawn with her eyes closed recounting, for me, the moment of her death. It was a truly beautiful experience that I shall never forget. She was at Omega that summer with her daughter Mindy and they were spending some quality time together. No one knew then that it would be her last summer.

The following summer, Mindy returned to Omega and I learned that her mother had made her final transit, in December, in a hospital in Philadelphia. Her actual death had been nothing like the imagined death we had acted out. Sarah was not surrounded by loved ones, nor was she able to thank them for what they had meant to her. But Sarah had already experienced her happy ending and she passed peacefully.

By giving myself the opportunity to create my own happy ending, I will be "fast-forwarding" to create the vision for it. Part of our women of worth work is about ending our lives to our own satisfaction and this is mind work.

Mind Moves

I was raised in an environment that stressed competition. Anything worth doing was worth doing well. That was my motto. Do your best, beat others, be first and always stand out from the crowd. As a result, I lost many opportunities to work harmoniously with my peers. I was too busy competing to be first.

It took many years of lonely searching for me to discover just how wonderful it is to work in harmony and be excited about doing my best as a contributing member of a group. It wasn't because I wanted to be the leader, or dominate or seize power, but because each member could grow a little more as a result of what I could contribute. And if I perceived that other group members surpassed me on any of the four levels of existence — physical, intellectual, emotional and spiritual — I could be happy for their success. This has been a serious mind move for me.

Sharmony - the result of a conscious mind move to do world work in a harmonious group of women.

The ability to be in *sharmony* and the opportunity to help to create it, has replaced my earlier alienating mindset. This is only the beginning of conscious mind moves I'm looking forward to experiencing as I consciously examine the workings of my mind and try to put sharmony into my later life.

Mind Work

As more women of worth join to explore the mind work of elderhood, they will come upon an igniting sense of purpose for their lives. The sleeping women will awaken and create a gentle revolution from within. They will cherish their tasks, as a sacred mission, and develop revolutionary plans to accomplish them.

Stimulating the mind, through journaling, reading or studying a new subject helps the emerging women of worth to evolve. Storytelling, either written or oral, is both personally and communally enriching. Women of worth can gather their stories, in the third millennium, and pass them on, as collective wisdom. They will be the future lessons to be taught in *herstory* classes.

Mindlessness

Minds need down time. There are some days when I wander throughout the spaces I call home, and talk to my plants or look at the paintings and let my mind drift. I have come to recognize this time as tired-mind time. The tired mind needs rest and refreshment just as the tired body demands it.

Recently I read a very challenging book on a subject that was new to me. I was into mind-stretch and intellectually exhausted when it was finished. Being an avid reader, I surprised myself by being unable to read anything serious for the next two days. When I realized that my mind needed recharging, I decided to focus on more physical activity. This ability to recognize a tired mind is a gift from my elder years. This new level of evolvement has allowed me to accept some passivity of mind as a positive and restorative process.

Selectiveness

Women of worth, who are able to develop a wisdom-loving mind, can experience an enriched mindstream. I have decided that, since I must live with my mind, I will create a mindstream worth living with in my later years. I have asked myself what is it that I would like to store in my conscious intellect?

As a conscious woman of worth, I know that I can program my intellect with material that assists in my enriched evolvement. How much intellectual programming time do we have in a day? How will we select the content for that programming time? What criteria will we use?

Richard Leviton is a medical researcher and author of a book entitled ***Brain Builders!: A Life-long Guide to Sharper Thinking, Better Memory and an Age-proof Mind***. It explores the "age-proof mind" and examines memory and sharper thinking. Leviton relates that doctors have examined the brains of ninety-year-olds and found them indistinguishable from the brains of twenty-year-olds. Our minds can continue to evolve. The fact that our minds are housed in bodies that have finite lifespans can encourage us to be extremely selective about what we, as women of worth, will use our minds to accomplish.

We could be content with the idea that we are all swim-

ming in a sea of ignorance and give voice to despair in our
elder years, or we can attempt to be the truth as we understand it with all of our limitations. We can give hope to the
world in our elder years. As a woman of worth in evolution,
I am learning each day to embody truth as I understand it for
me. I try to bring more mindfulness to each task before me.
As more and more women of worth bring mindfulness to
their lives, a larger intellectual consciousness will develop.

Speaking Your Mind

In her book, ***No Stone Unturned: The Life and Times
of Maggie Kuhn***, one of my favorite women of worth, talks
about how we can use our minds and voices:

Go to the people at the top—that is my advice to
anyone who wants to change the system, any system.
Don't moan and groan with like-minded souls. Don't
write letters or place a few phone calls and then sit
back and wait. Leave safety behind. Put your body
on the line. Stand before the people you fear and
speak your mind—even if your voice shakes. When
you least expect it, someone will actually listen to
what you have to say. Well-aimed slingshots can
topple giants. [4]

The slingshots of women of worth can empower the
world mind for good. The world needs she-elder mind.

During one of Maggie's final public appearances, she
needed assistance onto the stage as her aging body had be-

come very frail. Her mind, however, was as brilliant as ever. In order to get out of her chair to stand, Maggie rocked back and forth, using her cane to sustain momentum. She called this her "rock of ages." With wit and wisdom she addressed her audience. She has been an inspiration to many evolving women of worth.

Some of us will wish to speak our minds for good. Like Maggie Kuhn, some will speak in public arenas for the greater good of the community, while others will choose to interact one-on-one as living examples of the woman-of-worth mind at its best.

(1) Gail Sheehy, *New Passages: Mapping Your Life Across Time*, Random House, Inc: New York. 1995. pg. 419.
(2) Ibid., pg. 419.
(3) Ibid., pg. 419.
(4) Richard Leviton, *Brain Builders: A Lifelong Guide to Sharper Thinking, Better Memory, and an Age-proof Mind.* New York: Parker Publishing Company, 1995.
(5) Maggie Kuhn with Christina Long & Laura Quinn, *No Stone Unturned: The Life and Times of Maggie Kuhn.* Ballentine Books: New York. 1991. pg. 159.

Questions To Ponder About The Mind

1. Do I monitor the programming of my mind?

2. How would I define a mind stretch for myself?

3. Do I find myself thinking the same old ideas?

4. What happens when I speak my mind?

5. How have feminine archetypes influenced my thinking?

6. How can I get clear about what I still must learn in life?

7. How do I handle my tired mind?

8. What happy ending could I create for my life in my mind?

9. What mind moves would make my thoughts about my later years more positive?

10. What issues do I think she-elders might address, collectively, to empower the world mind for good?

4. Emotions

How can we silence the fear attached to she-elderhood?

As I speak with mature women, and discuss the topic with gerontology students in my classes, I am amazed at the number who express the fear that they will not have sufficient resources to complete their lives with dignity. Even those, who have planned and are presently comfortable, fear that they may outlive their resources.

We now know that toxic emotions, like fear and anxiety, lower our immune system. Learning to identify our toxic emotions can raise our emotional consciousness and make us less vulnerable to physical maladies as well. Our emotional literacy does not have to become a set of fixed responses but can evolve as we evolve into she-elderhood.

An important task for she-elders will be to work on eliminating those emotions that are toxic to their own lives. They may also wish to put some of their energy toward eliminating the root causes behind the societal toxins that create fear in women in their elder years. Our temperament is not our destiny and no human characteristic is beyond change. Emotional learning can be lifelong and we can set goals for ourselves on this consciousness level.

As I began this chapter I found my own emotions involved with a severe blizzard that was raging outside my window. I was terrified for all those who would not have a home in which to seek shelter. As I listened to the news I was heartened to hear the mayors of the major eastern cities discuss their plans for the homeless. I realized how much emotional energy I had focused on worrying about those who might be homeless and how grateful I was that I was not currently homeless. Having personally experienced temporary homelessness, due to a wild northeaster of a storm, I identify strongly with this fear. On a recent mid-term examination, when I asked my undergraduate students to name the one aging issue that they thought was most important, I was surprised that the majority named elder housing as the major issue. Becoming homeless again is one of my major fears. I use precious *shenergy* thinking about the possibility from time to time.

Shenergy - the collective energy of third millennial women.

The housing and care of aging women deserves national attention. When this issue is successfully addressed, and a national policy is in place that eliminates that fear for all women, then all that she-elder emotional energy can be freed up to be used in more positive ways both personally and collectively. This could be meaningful she-elder work.

Economics often silence the voices of many financially-secure, mature women causing them to emotionally detach from the less fortunate women in society. However, emotional detachment has its price. Fortunately, there are many wonderful women who work diligently to move the status of elder women forward.

Fear of abandonment by family and society, poverty, and homelessness in the elder years, are some of the negative emotions felt by women who have had the courage to break out of intolerable work or marriage situations. These same emotions are shared by women who have been abandoned by irresponsible spouses and women who have chosen to remain single.

If, in the next millennium, we can find a way to eliminate the "bag lady" fear, from she-elders in our society, we will have made a significant contribution toward magnifying the positive emotions of she-elderhood. I recently had an opportunity to visit with a widow in eastern Europe. She has lived most of her adult life in the same small apartment and she has been widowed for many years. She has never worked outside of her home. When her communist country transitioned to a democratic form of government recently, it was arranged for her to purchase her apartment at an affordable price. The government did not uproot her in her elder years. Because this government also has a national health care program in place she has no fear in her life. She knows that her needs will be taken care of until she transits this life.

I thought about what it would mean to have that kind of secure safety net under you as you age. It could help to eliminate the fear of being emotionally and financially abandoned. If small groups of more privileged she-elders, working in local geographic areas around the world, could commit to addressing this issue it could be eliminated. The possibility exists for the development of Sage-ing Centers around the world where elders could work through their collective and individual fears about aging in our society.

Hitting The Wall

By the time I had reached menopause I had hit the wall a number of times and developed some emotional resiliency. I had walked through some deep valleys and emerged on the other side. There had been many times, in the past, when I squandered my emotional energy and I regretted that. There had been times when I withheld emotional energy that should have been given away. But such was the confusion caused by my fear and lack of mindfulness. As a spiritual elder I have been willing to identify my fears, get as close to my fears as I can and bring mindfulness to them.

The whiplash generation of women, of which I am a part, are currently moving toward she-elderhood. They have had double messages most of their adult lives. This has produced a resiliency but also a lot of emotional confusion. Our society has changed the rules on us, so many times, that our heads are spinning. Spinning cuts down on the energy needed for forward movement. Since the energy needed to create the emotional essence of elderhood must be conserved, spinning must give way to a more intentional pattern of living. Our emotional essence must be focused if we are to model spiritual eldering for future generations.

Examining the flow of emotional energy into and out of our lives is an important task for the she-elder. If the flow is in one direction then we feel drained, and often angry, or depressed. If the flow is even, there is a synchronicity that is satisfying.

As a younger woman, I was not always conscious of the flow of my emotional energy. I often used this precious gift to supply others emotional needs, with no expectation of a re-turn flow of emotional energy. I remember times when my emotional well ran dry. I had nothing more to give. As a she-elder I am much more conscious of the flow of energy into, and out of, my life. I consider this consciousness to be one of the blessings of this time of my life.

The patriarchal rules, that dominated my younger life, expected me to be the eternal wellspring of emotional energy. Patriarchal rules also show that men don't want to see any diminution in women's nurturing instinct, even at that stage of life when such diminution would normally take place.

One of the least understood or least tolerated manifestations of the older woman's personality is her withdrawal from the abundantly other-directed behavior patterns of her mothering period, into a more self-directed mode of life, the change usually more or less coincident with menopause.

At this important turning point, many women openly express their intention to begin living for themselves, after years of self-abnegating devotion to husbands and/or children. Such women may return to school, take new jobs or hobbies, develop new kinds of friendships, cease to care whether men, find them attractive or not. A husband may feel uneasy about his aging wife's newfound independence, which he perceives (perhaps correctly) as a measure of indifference to his personal well-being. Grown children want their own independence. Yet, at the same time, they may feel psychicly abandoned by the mother who no longer centers her life around them, but instead pursues her own interests, which allow her little time for thinking of her offspring any more.[1]

At a recent seminar, one of the women commented that her children insisted on her remaining in the nurturing role of parent. She expressed her desire to be free of that responsibility and use that emotional energy for pursuits that she had to postpone while actively parenting her young. I reminded her that she was a parent-graduate, having successfully raised her children to adulthood. Parenting does not have to be lifetime commitment and, if we see it as such, we may need to spend some time journaling about why that might be so for us.

By the time we become she-elders we have learned that intergenerational conflict is universal and that to be in a conflict-free relationship is an oxymoron. Krisnamurti taught us that we are ultimately alone and it sometimes takes the she-eldering experience to appreciate aloneness.

The emotional abandonment of she-elders by others is an issue to be addressed. From what sources could she-elders expect to get their emotional energy needs met? One of the ways that women of worth can free up some of their emotional energy is by systematically forgiving. To forgive a person or thing, is not to condone the act but to free the energy that is bound in the process of maintaining animosity. Women of worth can little afford the luxury of expending useless energy.

If our anger is about present things happening to us then we must learn to communicate it now. If it is about old anger then we can deal with it in therapy or in journaling. This day never comes back so we don't want to pollute its' positive energy with past toxins.

When we become aware of the finitude of our emotional energy supply then negative emotions such as jealousy and anger are viewed very differently and seen as thieves of a very precious, but limited, resource.

Tonic Emotions

When we awaken our inner lover we can experience the ecstasy of loving ourselves which is Carol Ryff's first step toward happiness. Ryff, who is one of America's leading researchers on "happiness across the lifespan" is a psychologist and associate director of the Institute on Aging at the University of Wisconsin. Instead of focusing on the somewhat imprecise concept of happiness, Ryff studies psychological well-being. According to Ryff psychological well-being has six components: self-acceptance-feeling good about your past and present; autonomy-being able to follow your own convictions; mastery-having a sense of control over your daily life; positive relations-having trusting ties with others; purpose-having goals that give life meaning; and personal growth-having a sense of self-realization.

In a national, cross-cultural study of one thousand people, aged twenty-five to seventy, Ryff came up with what she calls a "phenomenal" finding: self-acceptance, like autonomy, does not diminish with age despite the ageist culture in which we live. Ryff found that purposefulness and personal growth do decline gradually for men and women, perhaps because society has not found creative ways to use the skills of older people. But two components of well being, mastery and positive relationships actually get better with age.[2]

Perhaps she-elders might address the issues of purposefulness and personal growth and find creative ways to use the skills of she-elders for their benefit and the benefit of our planet.

Through her writings and political action, Gloria Steinem has had a significant impact on the emotions of women in the second half of the twentieth century. She revealed some of her own emotional explorations in her writings and in so doing has enriched the literature for emerging women of worth.

For three years, ***Revolution from Within,*** the book that resulted from this exploring that began a few years after I turned fifty, was a living, breathing presence in my life. It helped me to know with certainty that our inner selves are no more important than an outer reality-but no less important either. Could I have learned this earlier? I don't know. Certainly, I would have been a more effective activist if I had. I would have been better able to stand up to conflict and criticism, to focus on what I could uniquely do instead of trying to do everything, and to waste less time confusing motion with action. But perhaps I couldn't explore internally until I stopped living in an external pressure cooker. Or perhaps I had to exhaust my self on half the circle before I could appreciate the other half. In a larger sense, it doesn't matter. The art of life isn't controlling what happens, which is impossible; it's using what happens.[3]

Emotional Intelligence

The art of she-eldering is not in controlling what happens, which is impossible, it is in using our emotional intelligence. Says Beatrice Bruteau, author of "The Unknown Goddess," an article in Shirley Nicholson's *The Goddess Reawakening*:

"If today's female archetype is to carry all of society forward," it must come laden with the richness of the male, "the fruits of rationality, intelligence and literacy."

Goddess mythology is reemerging in the late 20th century as the spiritual reflection of social change that has rapidly unfolded over the past 20 or 25 years. Millions of women all across the globe have expanded the bounds of their own evolution by growing into new roles previously occupied only by males. The result ought to be a reaffirmation of their feminine nature without a rejection of valuable skills once considered masculine.

"To hide behind the skirts of the Goddess and take shots at our male-dominated culture, however cleverly cloaked in scholarly erudition, is childish in the extreme," they conclude. Male or female, we must contact both the creative and destructive forces within each of us.

"We need to acknowledge and liberate the energies of the witchhunter, the murderer, the coward, the broken child, the starving child, who reside in us , not simply whine and point the finger at the bastions of neurotic male authority. Such transformation demands everything of us-our bodies, hearts, spirits, our softness and our hardness. The Goddess will not do it for us."

They are right. There is no going back to the Neolithic Goddess Age. Until we make war and weapons obsolete, we cannot recapture the innocent time before they were created. We must push our evolution forward by healing the relationships between women and men, conservatives and leftists, abuser and abused, pro-choice and pro-life.

The task before us is to create a new culture where feminine values are celebrated alongside positive masculine traits. Old Europe had one dramatic and fatal flaw: the inability to defend its civilization. The right balance of masculine and feminine values brings the creativity to create and the courage to defend.[4]

She-elders could be the ones to design and implement this new archetype and new world society of inclusion. The she-elder archetype will be a more complete woman in touch with her emotions both positive and negative. She will be emotionally intelligent. The "nurturing flow," the emotional flow, determines my environment. If the flow is positive the environment is healing and nurturing. If is negative it can be creative and push the frontiers of my emotions. If, however, it is too negative it can be very draining and even cause me to experience physical and mental illness.

The physical environment, around me, is important to the flow of my positive emotional energy. I have designed that environment to contribute to this positive flow. Alexandra Stoddard, in her inspiring book entitled *Living A Beautiful Life* gives us 500 ways to add elegance, order, beauty and joy to every day of our lives. She encourages us to create a physical environment that will bring forth positive emotions and thus enrich our emotional lives.[5]

The Sad Woman of Worth

It is most probably totally unrealistic to wish for nothing but fun-filled days. There are some days, in which I awaken with a black cloud hovering over me. I did not ask for it but there it is. It is on those days that I now know I have inner work to do. As a young woman I would withdraw and keep to myself when those gloomy days arrived. As a she-elder I have come to recognize the value of these days. I now mine them for the riches that they hold for my emotional evolution. I have gotten to the point where I can tell others that this is one of those days that I am working on my inner she-elder emotional life.

One day, as a thirty-five year old high school teacher, I walked into the faculty room and was greeted by my fellow teachers. An English teacher, who I now consider to be an important mentor for me, announced to the group that I was the "Pollyanna" of the high school. I knew "Pollyanna" was an upbeat character but I was not familiar with the true meaning of the story as was my friend. I, naively, thought it was a compliment at the time. My upbeat personality, and my reserve to bring cheer into the often morose faculty room, was being perceived as unreal. It was years later that I realized how important it is to be real and being real meant that there would be days when I hurt and I would be problem-solving.

On the other hand, I never wanted to be remembered as complaining and morose. I always limited my visits to the faculty room as I knew it was not a good use of my emotional energy. I chose not to give my valuable emotional energy to problems that were inevitable and recurring in high schools. When I look back now I have no regrets about doing that. Instead, I used that emotional energy, in positive ways, to create a model program for my students. Since then I have learned what it means to be perceived as a Pollyanna and the negative implications of that personality trait.

Most of my life I have been a pragmatist who wanted to work on solutions to problems not just complain about them endlessly. At this stage in my life I am teaching graduate gerontology courses. The literature, with which I work, is filled with accounts of the diminishments that occur with the aging process. Mourning those diminishments is an important part of emotional health. However, as I look back over my five decades of losses and subsequent mourning periods, I have learned that emerging from those periods is often exhilarating and creative.

The Sunny She-Elder

To stay in mourning is to miss the sunshine that could be brought into our lives and the lives of those with whom we interact. If we wish to be perceived as a sunny she-elder then we had best smile awhile. In recent years, the aging literature has documented the physical and emotional benefits of laughter.

I know she-elders who have decided that everyday will be "Funday." This may sound like an older version of Pollyanna but it may be light years ahead of its' alternative, a gloomy future. If we could buy happiness insurance no doubt many of us would be willing to make the investment. Making a fun plan could be a way to have some happiness insurance. We could add to our ability to find pleasure in each day. Putting fun into each day is important and it can be programmed into our schedules. It will create the balance so needed in the she-elder years.

Before moving to Houston I lived in an apartment building with a large number of mature adults. One of my goals, when I got into the elevator, was to say something humorous. If those left behind, when I walked down the hall to my apartment were still laughing, I felt wonderful and they did too. I considered that a good exchange of emotional energy.

Everyone gained something.

I have just begun to work on my next book that will be entitled **Spiritual Elders: People of Wit and Wisdom©** , and welcome any suggestions that you might want to share.

Creating the playful community among she-elders will be a glorious task for the future. Can you imagine the laughter and the energy that will flow? The enrichment of a humorous experience massages our emotions, often for weeks thereafter.

The Sacred Emotional Flow

The sacred is learning to discern what we are willing to spend our precious emotional energy on. Those issues that we are willing to embrace knowing that the flow will be uni-directional and worth the effort that it will take to address it. She-elders can learn that their precious emotional energy can move mountains and can create synergy in she-elder groups.

Given the time, consciousness and courage she-elders can push the edges of their existence and with that courage they can evolve emotionally. What a gift to give to ourselves and to the world! Positive emotional energy is a force that is needed and she-elders can make a meaningful contribution to that force. Learning to control the flow of negative energy, that comes forth from us, opens us to a whole new source of power and can free us from the pollutant of negativity in our lives. Monitoring this negative energy flow becomes more meaningful, as we mature, because there is the time and mind-fulness that we bring to the task.

Keeping a dream log has been very enlightening to me as

I struggle to understand my emerging she-elder emotions. I now can often interpret the dream very quickly and make decisions about the emotional issues. I have found that doing this work frees up that energy right away. The critical mass of the positive emotional energy of she-elders, in the third millennium, can impact the planet for the better. There will be enough of us who care and who have learned to conserve our energy and spend it only on issues for the greater good. She-elders will create the seamless flow. They will recognize the essential emotions that they will need for evolution. Deadened emotions will disappear as extraneous for their future evolution. Masks of illusion will no longer be needed because authenticity will make us feel so much better. The process of she-eldering will assist each of us to know who we have become and help us to monitor our evolving she-elderhood.

Sensitivity

Compassion will begin to emanate from us as we learn to sense the energy bodies of other she-elders. She-elder secrets often need to be shared in a compassionate group. She-elders, who have long ago jettisoned perfection as unrealistic, can bring sensitivity to the shared failings of other she-elders.

Caroline Heilbrun has been encouraging women to re-think their lives since 1979, when she wrote **Reinventing Womanhood**, a book describing the factors that prevent women from reaching "self-hood." The message that Heilbrun wants to leave with women is: "The point is to have an adventure, to do something else and realize that the struggle [itself] is the point."[6]

She-elder struggles have fortified us and many of us have figured out the central issue in our lives. We have figured out the negative patterns that we have repeated over and again and have conquered them to a degree. We know that we must do our own inner work, our own growth work as an important part of becoming a conscious she-elder.

Sharing

In the past few years I have had the opportunity to be in groups of she-elders, who were sharing their deepest life experiences. The insights that I gained from listening to them have given me positive energy. This amazing experience is synergistic. It has created very deep meaning where meaning may never have previously existed in my life. And it energizes the planet. It is the stuff of life. It is mystery and power shared. According to John Holmes, "The best exercise for the heart is to lift someone to a new level." She-elder sharing has the potential to lift generations to come to new levels.

During a seminar one of the participants shared about her experience of adopting a baby from a different culture. She and her husband began this experience with the highest motivation. Their hopes and dreams for their adopted son were to have him join with their biological children in a family where love and resources would be provided. Twenty years later she sits in tears from the unexpected pain that has come to her from this young adult. As I listened this could have been my story had my life drama not prevented my adopting a child. This could have been my pain and indeed it was. When thoughts of her life pass through my conscious awareness I send her positive spiritual and emotional energy. Her sharing has greatly enriched my life. But how often do we have an opportunity to share those really important issues in our lives in a supportive environment.

Gail Sheehy tells us that "Indeed, with our e-mail boxes and our fax and phone machines always "on," we have invaded our own solitude with an accelerated demand for immediate action and reaction. We seldom make time to process even the most meaningful experiences of our lives; we just speed through them.[7] Sheehy has called the years between age 45 to 65 the age of mastery. If women could master their emotional energy in the 45+ years what a rich resource they would have for their she-elderhood.

Taking she-elders to a new level of emotional evolution is the awesome task that lies ahead. Some of our life-processing can be done in the privacy of journaling or in the quietude of meditative moments but some must be done in a compassionate circle of she-elders. It is my dream that she-elders will develop women-of-worth circles that support them in their personal and collective evolutionary process.

(1) Barbara Walker, *The Crone: Women of Age, Wisdom and Power*. San Francisco: Harper, 1988. pg. 90.

(2) Judy Forman, Boston Globe, Feb. 20, 1995.

(3) Gloria Steinem, *Moving Beyond Words/ Age, Rage, Sex, Power, Money, Muscles: Breaking the Boundaries of Gender.* New York: Simon and Schuster, 1995, pg. 258.

(4) Patricia Aburdene & John Naisbitt, *Megatrends for Women, Villard Books,* 1992, pg. 263-4.

(5) Alexandra Stoddard, *Living A Beautiful Life*, New York: Avon Books, 1986.

(6) Kate Mulligan, Heilbrunian Adventures, AARP Bulletin, Vol. 37, No.2., pg.16.

(7) Gail Sheehy, *New Passages: Mapping Your Life Across Time*, New York: Random House, 1995. pg. 8.

Questions to Ponder About Emotions

1. How fearful am I of growing old? If not, why not?

2. What are my specific toxic emotions?

3. What can I do to eliminate my toxic emotions?

4. Are any of my fears universal fears?

5. How can my culture/ society handle my fears?

6. Do I examine the flow of emotional energy in and out of my life?

7. What are my emotional attachments to roles that I have out-grown?

8. From what sources can I expect to get my emotional energy needs met?

9. How can I increase the flow of tonic emotions into my life?

10. How do I envision my emotionally-evolved women of worth?

5. Spirit

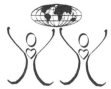

The "woman-of-worth spirit" is positive energy placed into the planet each day by those of us who consciously wish to serve the planet and enrich our own spiritual lives. This requires that spiritual energy be focused on personal, relational and world needs.

Upon realizing that a God defined is a God confined, women of worth can be open to what we personally experience as unlimited spirit in our lives. We can learn to respect the spiritual paths of our sisters. The woman-of-worth spirit is ever-evolving, spacious and non-confining. The spiritual essence within each of us invites a dialogue of devoutness to enliven its presence. I am hopeful that women of worth circles will form to facilitate this dialogue and to sustain it in the third millennium. What has developed recently among seminar leaders of the Spiritual Eldering Institute is an e-mail exchange of commentary about inspirational poems, books and music.

A woman of worth can express her spirit within current religious systems or search for a new path for her journey in the next millennium. She sees triumphalism as limiting, because it claims that "my way" is the only way to have spirit. This places the woman of worth in a box that confines even her spirit. Refusing to be confined, enlightened women of worth will continue to work to eliminate triumphalism in established religious traditions.

Some spiritual women of worth find meaningful spiritual work in leadership roles within contemporary spiritual traditions. But in the third millennium, the main issue will no longer be gender equality, but the transformation and evolvement of our religious institutions and the creation of new ones. Tolerance and inclusion will replace triumphalism, as our world shrinks and we learn to appreciate that which is good and beneficial for our world.

Today's spiritual women of worth know that this transition will create some confusion, but we also realize that painful and confusing as transitions often are, they are necessary to stretch us into a new and more fulfilling reality. Women of worth are currently working both from within and without established traditions. This collective work will create a critical mass in the next millennium. And with triumphalism beginning to be viewed historically, new expressions of the spirit will evolve.

Just as Thomas Merton taught us that there is no more justifiable warfare, feminist theologians, scholars and laywomen are now demonstrating and teaching that there is no more justifiable sexism in religion. The patriarchy is dying and will be dead in the third millennium. The male-dominated, shepherd technology, used to illustrate historic religious experience in the Judaic-Christian traditions, will give way to a gender-fair theology.

Within Religious Tradition

There are a number of women who prepared themselves

during the last quarter of the last century of the second millennium, and are presently leading congregations in established
spiritual systems. Many have come to these leadership roles
as second or third career opportunities. Some were denied
the opportunity as a first career choice.

Bernice Kimel Weiss, the mother of two, was ordained
as a rabbi at age forty-seven. "Even when I was young, I
thought about the rabbinate in religious life, " she says. Weiss
later commuted between Potomac, Maryland and New York
each week for four years to attend the Academy for Jewish
Religion. "Never say it is too late to start something new in
your life," she said during her ordination ceremony. Women
of worth can learn that it's never too late to start something
new in their spiritual lives.

The first phase of change within Judaism is already complete, explains Rabbi Ellen Dreyfus of Congregation Beth
Shalom in suburban Chicago, where women now serve as
rabbis and cantors. "Phase two will be transforming Judaism
to include women's perspectives and reflect women's lives
in ritual, theology, language and imagery," she says.[1]

Central to an enlightened woman's spiritual quest is
rejecting the assumption that God is male. While some
women feel empowered by envisioning God as the sacred
feminine, others insist divinity is neither female nor male.
Women of worth are seeking a rich new spirituality free
from male-imposed and/or self-imposed limits, metaphors,
language or interpretations.

The ordination of women is a measurable change in the

mainstream denominations. Of the 300 enrolled in Association of Theological Schools, more than 30 percent are women. These women students have appeared in significant numbers within the last quarter of the twentieth century, but their real impact will be felt in the third millennium as they change the spiritual systems from within.

The redrawn mission statements, emanating from organized traditions, will reflect women of worth leadership in evolving religious traditions. These seasoned leaders will seek a common spirituality that will extend beyond the walls of their respective institutions. Many spiritual women of worth have been working away at the sexism within organized religion in their own spheres. They have also been engaged in an assault on the teachings surrounding triumphalism and their alienating fallout. These two issues — sexism and triumphalism — have been brought into sharp focus in the last half of the twentieth century and hopefully will be eliminated in the third millennium.

One example is Maggie Kuhn, long time executive in the Presbyterian Church:

> When I was thirty, I became a church deacon, a new position for a woman to assume in those days. Later, I was nominated to become the first woman on the session, the church's governing body. Though the Presbyterian church had allowed women to become church elders since 1930, many individual churches did not accept the idea. In those churches, women were confined to dusting the sanctuary and

raising funds. The pastor of First Presbyterian was among those who felt church business was a man's job. On the day my name was put forth, he stood before the group assembled to hear the nominations and in a booming voice said, "No! As long as I am pastor of this church, there will be no woman on the session." I felt as if I had been slapped in the face. At first I was mortified — and then furious. This incident built up in me a well of resentment against the church's backwardness. My father, who was on the session himself, was shocked that I would not be able to follow in his footsteps as a church elder. [2]

I had a similar experience. As a fledgling minister's wife, years ago, I was asked to be president of the Women's Association in our first congregation. Although it was a small, rural congregation, I felt a sense of significance in that role. However, I was soon to learn that the Women's Association was primarily a fund-raising group without real policy-making influence. By the time I was a seasoned minister's wife in our third, large, suburban congregation, I no longer wanted to be a member of the Women's Association. I wanted to be an elder on the ruling board. When I asked about that possibility, I was discouraged from having my name placed in nomination. I was told that it would be a conflict of interest with my role as minister's wife. I realized then that I had been placed in a role that limited me. Since I had accepted the role of minister's wife at great personal sacrifice and had already given many years of service in almost every other position, I found it difficult to understand how being an elder could be considered a conflict of interest. The only conflict of interest I could see would be my participation in decisions about the pastor's salary. I certainly would have excused myself from that particular discussion.

Although I was denied access to the main ruling board in the congregation, I was able to encourage my husband to propose to the session that a young woman be hired as assistant pastor. She was the first female to serve, in a pastoral role, in our Presbytery. She served on the frontlines of the female ministerial invasion that was soon to follow in the 1980s.

In the 1970s and early 1980s, women in the contemporary choir, of which I was a member, took absolute delight in changing all references to God in the hymns to the feminine form. It was a joyful, celebratory time in worship and we somehow knew that our collective raised consciousness would make lasting changes in worship. What we were experiencing, for the first time, was only the beginning of a much greater spiritual consciousness awaiting us in the future.

While attending Princeton Theological Seminary with my first husband, in the early sixties, I started working on ecumenical issues, as they were called at that time. The words interfaith and trans-denominational also describe this work and are in common usage now. Since that time I have been working at building interfaith bridges.

In the early seventies, I was privileged to be a member of a congregation with bright, energetic, spiritually-charged people. Both the community and congregation were undergoing profound sociological changes. When my husband and I arrived in that community, we found the charred ashes of a recently burned church building instead of a sanctuary. A year later, on the Sunday when our new sanctuary was being dedicated, the street in front of the church was lined with state police. They were there to assure that the protest going on in the community that day would remain peaceful. The Jewish Defense League was marching across the town, protesting the recent burning of a cross on a local lawn by the Ku Klux Klan. That was just the beginning. In this charming town we would experience all the prominent social issues of the times—racism, sexism and triumphalism. The fourteen years that I spent with this community are etched indelibly in my memory. I was privileged to be a part of a community of faith that worked hard for social change and over time saw tangible results.

In her thought-provoking book, ***Standing Again at Sinai: Judaism From a Feminist Perspective***, Judith Plaskow talks about her unwillingness to repudiate the instruction of her parents and well-meaning and dedicated teachers. I share this thinking with her. I too want to save that which was helpful and good and served as a boundary that kept me from harm. However, that which has been limiting needs to be revisioned. She shares some of her observations:

> Reform always begins in conviction and vision.
> Jewish feminism, like all reform movements, is rooted
> in deeply felt experience and a powerful image of

religious change. Wherever the individual feminist locates her active interests—in liturgy, theology, midrash, law—she acts out of commitment to an animating vision that has important repercussions for community life and practice. My central reason is to articulate one version of this vision and to foster its growth. If feminist theologies help to reanimate the connection between practice and belief in the Jewish world more generally, they will have made another important contribution to Jewish religious life.[3]

Judith Plaskaw has so eloquently articulated one version of an animating vision. I too wish to add my version and be open to the new and inspiring versions of other women.

We have heard that old saying "inch-by-inch life's a cinch, yard-by-yard life is hard." And so, if inch-by-inch life is a cinch, then socially-conscious and spiritually-alive congregations can choose to address the issues inch-by-inch. As we enter a new millennium women of great worth are expressing their spirituality through service within religious traditions and inch-by-inch they are making a difference.

Outside Religious Traditions

Since total-system transformation may be a long time coming in many religious traditions, and women are interested in their current spiritual lives, some are choosing to pursue spirituality outside the mainstream. More than 150 groups of United States Catholics and Protestants worship in all-female clusters in private homes and on college campuses. Collectively this network calls itself Women-Church. A Women-Church International Conference pulls them together and states its mission as reinterpreting the language, symbols and texts of Christianity to serve women's spirituality. These women wish to develop a new understanding of church, create meaningful worship experiences and conserve the energy that it takes to fight existing institutions.

Spiritual Shock Waves

Around the time of his fiftieth birthday my husband of twenty-eight years had a serious mid-life crises, I knew that he had experienced a lot of headaches and was not very happy with himself but I thought it was just another life transition and that it would pass in time. Then one day in May he came home and announced that he wanted a divorce. At first, I thought it was a joke and told him that divorce was not a subject to kid about. He then let me know that he was serious and I could not believe what I was hearing. The word divorce had never been mentioned in our home and we rarely argued. I thought that we had a very solid marriage and, although there were some pieces missing for both of us, I felt that our marriage was a good one. When the shock settled in I was inconsolable. Everything that I had lived for was crumbling about me. Most importantly, I felt that we would be setting a very bad example for the congregation by divorcing and not working on reconciliation. After a year of struggling to save our marriage I was emotionally and spiritually drained. He had made a unilateral decision to divorce and it impacted the lives of hundreds of people who cared deeply about our family. Many of my precious life dreams, like having a fifty year marriage and a solid family, disappeared during that year.

A few months after our divorce he called to tell me that he was marrying one of the members of our congregation and taking her with him to his new congregation. I wished him well with his new call to a small congregation a thousand miles away.

The next year he called to tell me that his new marriage was not working and that neither he nor his new wife were happy. They both wished themselves back in their former marriages. He asked if I would consider remarriage and I agreed to explore the idea. When he approached his session with the possibility of divorcing his new wife and remarrying me he met with resistance. One of the female Elders, who had been recently divorced, said that she could not tolerate the upset that the minister's divorce would cause to herself and the congregation.

When he called to share with me the reaction of his session he had already decided to stay with his new wife. Not wanting to upset a second congregation I agreed that his decision was probably the best one. Remarriage will be, for me, the road not taken—as the famous poem concludes—and maybe it has made all the difference.

As the role of minister's wife fell away I realized that a huge block of time opened for me. At first I was lost without the role but, a few months later, I realized that I had gained a new freedom. I was now free to pursue my own spiritual

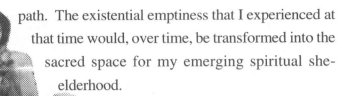

On our way to church. Elizabeth Moriarty, Betty Anne, Joan, Joe & Row

path. The existential emptiness that I experienced at that time would, over time, be transformed into the sacred space for my emerging spiritual she-elderhood.

During that time of desolation, when all that I had valued was questioned, there was always the temptation to look back to a more secure spiritual time. Sometimes I wished myself back in the comfort of the Roman Catholic Church where I had been for the first twenty-four years of my life. There was strong family and community support for my faith in those days and I missed that support.

Too embarrassed to worship with our own congregation and wishing to put the public pain of the divorce behind me, I began worshipping with my neighbors, Alan and Susan, who were Quakers. In their quiet and unassuming fashion they surrounded me with love that was very restorative. The simplicity of the Quaker worship was a balm for my wounded spirit.

As my spiritual worldview broke up over the next ten years, I became a member of three very different reformed congregations. When I joined the first congregation I remained at the fringe of the congregation. I wanted to view it almost as an outsider. Although I participated in weekly worship and financially supported the church I remained in a detached observer mode. The Associate Pastor was a friend of mine and she protected me from the many committees seeking my help. She knew that I needed time to heal.

When a professional relocation permitted me to join a second small, rural congregation I became more involved. I admired the female pastor and the difficult task she had in leading this tiny congregation. A few years later another professional move gave me an opportunity to join a third congregation. This time it was a very large, sophisticated suburban congregation fraught with infighting and pastor-bashing. Although I met some very wonderful people within that congregation I still felt spiritually lost.

I concluded that there was no longer a comfortable fit for me in organized religion. I was greatly saddened about that as organized religion has taken a great deal of my dedication and spiritual energy for more than forty years. My mid-forties to mid-fifties were a very unsettled time for me spiritually. I began worshiping with a variety of congregations including the Congregationalists, the Unitarians, the Methodists, the Roman Catholics and many other non-Christian religious traditions. I was searching on the outside for what, I know now, can only be found within.

There were many anxious moments in that decade. My search took me in many directions as I looked for a more mature expression of the spirit emerging from within me. I was already in my fifties when I learned from Reb Zalman how to look for the pearls in those anxious moments. I wish I had known how to do that in my forties. In more recent years I have journaled about that time of my life and I have looked for and found the pearls that were hidden in those anxious moments. Those pearls were part of my own personal spiritual evolvement. I had to move past those anxieties of the spirit into a depth experience. Now, I no longer fear the anxious moments but realize, that if I stay with them, they will bring me to new place of spirit.

The divorce has been the most severe shock wave to hit me and it has left me with the knowledge that my spirit is strong. This evolving spirit may be tested but it will be lead to the resources that will continue to sustain it throughout elderhood. It will endure whatever shock waves come.

The Spiritual She-Elder Archetype

In the early nineties, as I was preparing for a seminar presentation at the Spiritual Eldering Institute in Philadelphia, I began to realize how inadequate the old femimne

She-Elder Archetype - in process and may take a milleniumn to form.

archetypes were for me, a woman ripening into elderhood in the third millennium. I began to look closely at these archetypes and opened up the issue for discussion at the seminar.The icons from the past and the images of feminine spirituality did not fully express the contemporary woman-of-worth faith that was evolving for me. This faith could be reflected in some of these images but was, somehow, much more than all of these archetypes taken together.

The historic feminine archetypes such as the goddess, Gaia, wisewoman, healer, crone, white witch, and Celtic priestess, etc. could each be a part of my expression of feminine spirituality but, individually, they would be only a part of it. None of these archetypes can fully represent the emerging woman-of-worth spirit. This is unique in history and, therefore, will need a more complete archetype that expresses this uniqueness.

Perhaps emerging women of worth can draw on these historical images for inspiration in forming a new archetype for our collective future. The third millennial women of worth will mark tracks in uncharted territory and our spiritual lives will flow into all the universe.

Spiritual Consciousness

Spiritual growth is an area that some of us may set aside, half hoping the day will come when some soul-stretching, cathartic experience will lift us out of our ordinary consciousness for a glimpse of the sacred and eternal. However, as an emerging woman of worth, I have found that the raising of spiritual consciousness is integral to my life and can no longer be postponed for another day. The time I spend in meditation is time for the positive charging of my spiritual batteries and precious time for sending positive energy into our planet. It is as life-sustaining as the food I eat.

Becoming a woman of worth is primarily a process of spiritual growth. Instead of focusing on our time as running out, we should mark the moment. The present never ages. Each moment is like a snowflake: unique, unspoiled, unrepeatable. The present moment can be appreciated for its uniqueness and element of surprise. Because the present moment is inherently different from past moments, each day can become an awakening. As spiritual consciousness evolves, growth continues. Waking up to higher and higher levels of spiritual consciousness is a gift we can give ourselves. Raising our spiritual consciousness can positively impact the quality of our elderhood.

Sacred Space

I recently visited an old friend who has a devout faith in an orthodox tradition. As I sat in her dining room, I noticed the statue of the Infant of Prague mounted near the ceiling in one corner of the room and a red electric candle burning before it. I listened attentively as she explained the importance of that icon in her life. Suddenly, I felt a deep sense of loss. I had dismissed all of my icons long ago, but now I wished for something tangible to help express the woman-of-worth spirit within me. As a result, I decided to develop my own sacred sanctuary and to incorporate whatever objects would inspire my spirit. This vision became a reality in Houston.

I have been a lifelong gardener and have lovingly nurtured large outdoor spaces that have rewarded me with great beauty and raised my spirit level. However, now I live in a patio home, which is just right for an active empty-nester. I have a small, totally private, contemplative garden with a mini-waterfall. My plants have names and are considered part of my spiritual family. One large shefelera plant is named "Bar-Dor-Rosie-Penny," in honor of the four colleagues who gave it to me when I resigned from the directorship of the

Suffolk County Respite Care Program. Another plant came from my brother Joe, from California, to celebrate my marriage to Ivan. A rosemary bush, from my oldest daughter Lisa, fills the space with welcoming scent. A very special ivy was brought to me by my sister Joan, from my late father's garden. A prayer plant, given to me by my father two years before he passed, has had a death and resurrection every year for the past twenty years. Just when it looks like it has perished, it starts sending up new shoots. I also invite seasonal plants of scent and color to brighten the environment and join the Happy Buddha figure that smiles up at me each morning. My sacred space is serene, green, quiet, sunny, scented and special.

Mother Mary Cornelia, Mother Superior, Order of the Immaculate Heart of Mary.

I have also assembled a tray of special meditation items. A small silver bell, with a llama figure as the handle, was a gift from my grandaunt Cornelia, who passed many years ago but continues to be a mentoring figure for me. She started a girl's school in Lima, Peru in the 1930s and provided significant leadership at a time in history when few women were able to distinguish themselves. She began the education of young women in that part of the world. We know that an educated womanhood can be a significant blessing on the planet. Other items on my tray include special stones from friends and grandchildren, and candles of many colors that I light when focusing my spiritual energy on a certain chakra. My silver baby cup is there to remind me that I am blessed to be a blessing. There's also a small chime that I use to begin and end seminar sessions and times of meditation. It is a very special gift from my spiritual sisters, Steffi and Elizabeth. The mix of items changes from time to time, hopefully mirroring and enhancing my spiritual evolution.

My seat is a small wooden bench with a soft pillow. I place my shawl around my shoulders on chilly mornings and bless the warmth of the sun when it is shining. I meditate in my sacred space each morning to refresh the spirit within.

For her sacred space, Elizabeth has decorated a room that once belonged to one of her five grown children. She has created a special place for herself that reflects the deep connectedness she feels with native Americans. Her walls are covered with artifacts, like her drum collection, that have special meaning for her. She uses her drums to create beats that help to center her spirit. On the floor, in the center of the room, is a hand-painted floor covering on which Elizabeth sits. Her sacred space is in earth tones. It is a warm place in which to raise spiritual consciousness. Elizabeth also has a collection of Judaic books and art that have enriched her spiritual life.

Elizabeth David, Steffi Shapiro and Betty Ann Sullivan. April 1996

Steffi, a Yoga instructor, prefers the simplicity of uncluttered space. Her sacred space is open. She sits on the floor on a pillow. She uses ting shaw bells and expresses her spirituality through yoga and dance.

The sacred spaces I have just described reflect the spirit

of each woman and her unique approach to raising her spiritual consciousness. We are very different people and express our spirituality in different ways. As women of worth, we wish to be fully alive to what raises our spirits.

Silence

The power of she-elder silence can be awesome. I set aside some time everyday to experience silence. It is a gift to myself. From this silence has come inspiration, rest for my mind, and a chance just "to be." To experience "being-ness" is a rich experience that I have allowed myself as an emerging elder. I have come to cherish this time of silence.

The bible says, "Be still, and know that I am God." Stilling the mind and body is a powerful tool for women of worth. It can bring a blessing to us and to our planet. Once we connect to our inner essence, we can connect to mystery. This is often accomplished by remaining very still and focusing on your breath while clearing the mind of intruding thoughts.

Silent meditation, as taught by the Buddha, is an art of living. He never established or taught any religion or "ism." He never instructed those who came to him to practice any rites or rituals, any empty formalities. Instead, he taught them just to observe nature as it is, by looking to the reality inside. Such action can only be positive, creative and helpful to ourselves and others.

Over the past year, I have begun a walking meditation in a local park. It's a great way to accomplish something good for my body while doing my inner spiritual work. Most mornings, my friend Billie and I walk in silence through the park. This special time in my day has not only brought a new joy into my life, but has brought new health and fitness to my body.

Do I Have A Religious Preference?

When I took a world religions course at Princeton Theological Seminary in the early sixties, I knew, in my heart of hearts, that I had a religious preference. It was a very comfortable time, but times have changed for me. My path is not that straight and certainly not that narrow.

A year after we were married, I accompanied my husband Ivan to the emergency room of a Boston Hospital. While he was being treated, for congestive heart failure, I was asked to fill out the forms needed for his admission. The nurse asked me to fill in our religious preference on the intake form. As I heard myself saying the words, "No preference," I couldn't believe what I was hearing.

Was this the woman who had spent twenty-four years of her life as a devout Roman Catholic, three years with her first husband at Princeton Theological Seminary, twenty years as a minister's wife, a decade exploring a variety of spiritual paths and five years studying with a Rabbi? Indeed, it was that woman.

At the time of the question from the emergency room nurse, I was too preoccupied with Ivan's condition to give much attention to it. But as he became well again, I found myself pondering my response on that anxious day. I thought about how far I had come from my narrow interpretation of spirit, as clothed in specific traditions, to my much wider understanding of spiritual energy. I found myself wanting to speak to the emergency room nurse, telling her that I considered myself a deeply spiritual person — indeed a high-level spirit — but that I was no longer grounded in any one tradition. I preferred to be free to draw from all of them as the spirit provided.

Do I have a religious preference? The answer is still no. My spirituality is a very personal spirituality. I was born into the Christian tradition and, for much of my life, Jesus has been my master teacher. I have learned truth from his teachings and I am very grateful for that grounding. With the post-triumphalistic thinking that has impacted this period of my life, I have learned the importance of trying to understand and respect another person's truth. We all see through a glass darkly. Are there any among us who have the whole truth?

Am I comfortable in many traditions? The answer is yes. Will I need to find another label in order to identify my spirituality? The answer is no. That will not be necessary as my spirituality is woven through every moment of my life. I now know that my she-elder spirituality cannot be confined. A God-spirit defined is a God-spirit confined. I have decided that my spirituality does not need a specific label.

Do I desire to be in community with other spiritual people? Yes, and I have joined a congregation in Houston in search of that community. This congregation lives the social gospel and impacts the major social issues in northwest Houston.

Following a church service recently, my husband Ivan lost consciousness again and the medics were called. He refused to be hospitalized, so I did not get to answer the emergency room questions again. However, I found that my reaction to this recent illness was very different from my reaction three years earlier. As soon as he was stabilized, I e-mailed Steffi in Boston and asked her to send spiritual energy to him. She e-mailed me back that she was sending Reiki healing energy. Our female pastor also gave spiritual energy to Ivan and he is presently is good health.

So where do we get spiritual energy? We get it from within and from others who have raised their consciousness about spiritual energy. I look forward, with great expectation, to years of sharing with women of worth in my own spiritual community. I also look forward to meeting other women of worth throughout the world. The deep spirituality of later life can give meaning and purpose to those years. What could be better than using this earthly experience to evolve as a spiritual woman of worth?

(1) Patricia Aburdene and John Naisbitt, *Megatrends for Women*, New York: Random House Inc. 1992. pg. 118.
(2) Maggie Kuhn with Christina Long and Laura Quinn. *No Stone Unturned: The Life and Times of Maggie Kuhn*.New York: Ballentine Books, 1991. pg. 93
(3) Judith Plaskow, *Standing Again at Sinai: Judaism from a Feminist Perspective*. San Francisco: Harper, 1991, p.23.
(4) Gail Sheehy, *New Passages: Mapping Your Life Across Time*. New York: Random House, Inc. 1995. pg. 428.

Questions To Ponder About Spirit

1. What would my personal sacred spiritual space be like?

2. What special objects or icons would I bring into my spiritual space?

3. How can I use my spiritual energy to enrich the planet?

4. What can I, as a woman of worth, do to raise my spiritual consciousness?

5. Do I have a religious preference?

6. How do I feel about triumphalism?

7. How has triumphalism impacted my spiritual worldview?

8. Do any of the historic feminine archetypes inspire me spiritually?

9. How important is a spiritual community in my life?

10. How would I describe my ideal spiritual woman of worth?

6. Lifestyle

Thoreau tells us in Walden Pond why he retreated from life for a period of time: "I went to the woods because I wished to live deliberately, to front only the essential facts of life and see if I could learn what it had to teach and not, when I came to die, discover that I had not lived." While it may not be necessary to take to the woods or other place of sanctuary to "live deliberately," there is some merit to simplifying our lives. By lightening our load, the energy we would have given to caring for "things" can be freed up for developing our roles as women of worth.

Simplifying may seem to contradict the basic concept of women of worth being more highly valued than the elderly traditionally are. After all, being valued in society normally means being busy as consumers, acquiring more goods and services. Shouldn't we want to be considered even more of a potential target market by manufacturers and corporations? But do we really want our existence to be purely for economic purposes?

It remains for this feminist wave to create viable substitutes for the patriarchal values underlying the economics of our society. It won't be easy. We have to make what's wrong visible before it will be moved aside. By realizing that our rebellion will help balance the world's consumption, we'll be more willing to rebel against our traditional role of managing consumption, whether as a homemaker or career woman.[1]

This possible change is consumption patterns bodes well for women of worth, as we learn to be less wasteful. Living culturally rich, but consumption-restrained life styles, will provide graphic examples for future generations to emulate. The "greedy geezer" label, synonymous with members of earlier generations, may become obsolete for future elders.

As I approached my fifties, I began to see my possessions as stumbling blocks to my mind, body, spirit and emotional evolution. So I gave most of them to my children or friends, or sold them in a yard sale. When I was between marriages, I had the opportunity to spend a year of my life living in a small cell of a room with little more than the work and leisure clothing I needed. I now refer to that period as my "sanctuary period." When I made the decision to try to live simply, I had no idea this time would be so valuable or that my emotional growth would be worth the sacrifice. It was a most profitable experience, as it taught me a lot about my inner and outer needs.

Because I was living so minimally during that sanctuary year, many hours were freed up for journaling, meditating, reading, thinking and just being with myself. It opened up hours to take walks with friends or listen to recordings of symphonies. During that year, I was able to create a list of the very few possessions I might invite back into my life and those I would never miss. It helped me discern which things would give added value and which would add clutter to my existence.

Although I treasure the many teachings I garnered about my physical needs during the sanctuary period, I even more deeply appreciate what I learned about my essential emotional needs. I learned that privacy and quiet are important to me because they set the stage for doing my inner woman-of-worth work. For example, while I shared a bathroom with a very congenial suitemate, I did miss my privacy. I realized that sharing toileting made me anxious.

The small room that I occupied, was really all the space I physically needed, but it didn't meet another important emotional need: a view of nature. I now live in a small patio home, but every room has a lovely scenic view that changes with the seasons.

My mother used to tell me, "Be careful what you let into your life because the more stuff you have, the more stuff has you." She was right. I often heard those words running through my mind in my nest-building period, but I didn't always follow that sage advice. When my twenty-eight-year marriage ended, I had to decide what to take with me into my new townhome. After careful deliberation, I decided to choose only those things that would bring joy into my life. Many of the other things I remember packing and unpacking through many moves, some never having been used—not even once. They had been totally useless and did not satisfy my needs at any level.

My Mother,
Elizabeth
Catherine
Moriarty

Consciously collecting, as I have come to call the process of inviting things into my life, has been raised to an art form for me. I currently live with as few possessions as possible. I am very conscious about what I will allow into my life. I am also very conscious about consuming only what I need, and no more. It is a lifestyle choice that is bringing satisfaction to me as a woman of worth. This may not meet the emotional needs of all women of worth, but there's value in taking a conscious inventory of our material needs.

In her guide to scaling down and enjoying more, entitled ***Living the Simple Life***, Elaine St. James tells us to remember that relationships take time.

> When you're zeroing in on what's important to you, keep in mind that close relationships frequently need more time than we've devoted to them in recent years. All the major world religions tell us to love one another, but when our lives become so cluttered with things to care for that we have little time to reach out to people or animals.[2]

Kittikins blessed our
family for many years

Tꞏe Seven Generation View

My children experienced two very different grandfathers. Upon entering his retirement years, one grandfather bought a very large home for himself and his second wife. The maintenance of this property required a lot of time and money. He spent his elder years caring for his handsomely landscaped three-acre property, although he could have afforded to pay for these services. He had, in effect, created another full-time job for himself in order to keep busy. As a result, he was rarely available to participate in the lives of his grandchil-

Rowland T.
Moriarty

dren. He often declined invitations to their school plays and important concerts. When he died, not much of him lived on in his grandchildren. They rarely speak of him.

Their other grandfather had both a winter home and a summer home to maintain, but these homes were much less pretentious and easier to care for. This gave him time to participate in the lives of his seven grandchildren. In fact, he maintained the summer home primarily as a gathering place for his grandchildren because he wanted to spend some time with each of them. Although it has been many years since this grandfather died, his seven grandchildren speak lovingly about him every time they are together. He had a durative view of life. His values lived on in succeeding generations. So who was the really wealthy grandfather?

With his grandchildren at "Beachy-Beach," his summer home.

Nesting

"We hear much about women's nest-building instincts, but hear little of any nest-destroying behavior. As represented by several versions of the Crone, older women may experience strong urges to simplify their lives such as by weeding out possessions, moving to smaller quarters and keeping them neater, or restricting their social contacts to a few good friends instead of a wide circle of acquaintances. They may give things away, neglect their houses, stop buying clothes. They may still be consumers, but only in respect to a personal enthusiasm, such as a collection.

Earlier societies apparently understood more about the nest-destroying stage. Kali's of both sexes were expected to retire from participation in the life of clan and community for one or more retreat periods, after they married and raised their

> The Hindu mother goddess, the wife of Shiva, is known by many names and many forms. Kali is her name as the goddess suffering. Suffering, as the followers of Kali point out, is a very real part of life.

children. Some would leave their families and possessions behind for good, simplifying existence down to the bare necessities. Alone in the forest, or in anchorite communities, they would turn their attention toward the oncoming end of life. Through introspection, they would seek revelation of the world's ultimate meaning, or lack thereof. For [Hindus], this final stage of life's activity is referred to as *moksha* or "liberation," and is also called "the art of dying." [3]

The Search For Balance

Workaholism has been given social acceptance in the United States and some other parts of the first world. We can create such busyness in our lives that we don't give ourselves the time it takes to really learn the lessons we're supposed to learn in this life.

When I married my husband Ivan in my mid-fifties, I was

again faced with a household of accumulated goods —things my new husband had acquired during his thirty-eight year marriage to his wife who had passed a year before we met. He and Franciska had immigrated to Canada, after escaping at night during the Hungarian revolution. They arrived in Canada with the clothes on their backs and nothing else. Through hard work and careful saving, they made a good life for themselves and their family. So when I first brought up the idea of thinning out his possessions, he seemed very puzzled. Why would anyone want to get rid of those things they had spent a lifetime acquiring? I was asking him to look through his lifetime collection of earthly treasures and make some decisions about whether he could live without them and still be happy. He decided that he could live without a lot of them, and many boxes were prepared for our daughters and the grandchildren.

Ivan and I have been married three years now. We are still finding things to give away. Now Ivan understands the benefit of traveling lightly upon the earth. When I ask my beloved husband if he has missed anything that we gave away, he gets a twinkle in his eye and says, "Not yet." We both understand simplification . We appreciate how it has given us more time for each other and the meaningful projects on which we wish to spend our elder energy.

(1) Gail Sheehy, *New Passages: Mapping Your Life Across Time*. New York: Random House, Inc. 1995. pg. 239.
(2) Elaine St. James, *Living the Simple Life*. New York: Hyperion, 1996, pg 91.
(3) Barbara Walker, *The Crone: Women of Age, Wisdom and Power*.San Francisco: Harper. 1988. pg. 9.

Questions to Ponder On
Lifestyle

1. What possessions will be important to keep throughout my life?

2. Do I consume more than I really need to consume?

3. What will I have to rearrange in my life to create balance?

4. Will my lifestyle choices impact the planet positively or negatively?

5. What would my ideal woman-of-worth "nest" be like?

6. Why would I, as a woman of worth, want to simplify my life?

7. What nesting needs are necessary to support my emotional life?

8. What nest-destroying feelings have I experienced?

9. How could I use time and energy that's freed up by simplification?

10. Will my present lifestyle allow me to spend time with the important people in my life?

7. New Roles

In our post-menopausal years, it is important to ask ourselves, "What will I do to give meaning and purpose to the years of life that I have left?" It is even more important to answer that question to our satisfaction. It is our chance to place new opportunities before us and make significant choices. Ruth Harriet Jacobs' book entitled *Be An Outrageous Older Woman: A R-A-S-P (Remarkable Aging Smart Person)* raised my consciousness about the need to work on changing society's perception of mature women. The world has not yet recognized our value. That's because it has never seen so many healthy, educated, caring, concerned women of worth before. We are one of the world's precious resources that will be discovered in the third millennium.

The answer to the question about how we will spend our post-menopausal years is going to take work. We must perceive and create roles for ourselves that value and support the issues of elder women. And by making choices that are good for us, individually and collectively, everybody wins. Society benefits from having more active and productive members. As valued contributors, we'll receive resources from society that will allow us to do more. And we'll feel better about ourselves.

The economics of life are a reality that cannot be escaped.

Ruth Harriet
Jacobs

This mass movement of women demanding a valued place in society will produce equity. Their collective raised consciousness will bring an examination of the shared fears and can produce solutions. The critical creative mass of she-elders will work to overcome the resistance to be valued, from within themselves and from our patriarchal society. I envision it as a "gentle revolution."

Maggie Kuhn, founder of the Grey Panthers, gave her time to monitor the media regarding the image of elders that was being portrayed to the world. She saw elders as performing five important roles: mentor, mobilizer, monitor, motivator and mediator. It will take women in all of these roles to bring a purposeful and valued vision to women of worth.

> One of the activities of The Grey Panthers is to monitor the media.

In a research paper entitled "Expanding Social Roles for Older Women," Dr. Jacobs takes a more detailed look at roles, identifying ten major ones for mature women:

Nurturers. Women who define themselves, primarily, as caregivers to others — wives, mothers, grandmothers, volunteers, secretaries and other workers who nurture bosses.

Unutilized nurturers. Women whose nurturing roles have been lost, often through widowhood or divorce.

Re-engaged nurturers. Often women who have become volunteers, teachers, or social workers after children leave home.

Chum networkers and recreation-oriented women. Women, who may be married, employed or not-employed, for whom hobbies, travel, and/or friendships come first.

Careerists. Employed and unemployed women who find their primary identity through paid work.

Seekers. Women in transition between roles or women who are perpetually looking for something to change because their lives are unsatisfying.

Faded beauties. Women who dedicate themselves to mourning the loss of their youthful appearance or trying to preserve it.

Illness-oriented women. Unhappy older women seeking attention from healers, within and out-side of the professional medical community.

Escapists and isolates. Women who seek solace through drugs or alcohol. These women are often rejected by their families and by society and thus, become isolated. They may also be rejected, because others don't want to be confronted with the future they fear for themselves.

Advocates and assertive women. Women who work to make society better for themselves, other older women and the world at large. [2]

We might embody some of these roles. The important task is getting clear about which roles have become obsolete for us and which are no longer appropriate for us as emerging women of worth and what percentage of each role will en-hance our women of worth mix. Although this is a personal task to be achieved by each of us, it's important to open up a dialogue around the issue of role development as a means of supporting this activity.

But the key is, we do have choices; we don't have to accept what others choose for us and we can change what we've chosen for ourselves.

When I conceived my first child, in 1960, I purposefully took on the role of parent. At that time, I thought the role would last forever. Once a mother, always a mother was my thinking.

I remember the meltdown that transpired between my oldest daughter, Lisa, and me when she came home from college, in her senior year, and asked if we could be friends. Essentially she was telling me that she had reached the point in her maturing process, when she was ready to be treated as an adult. She wanted our parent-child relationship to end. Unable to really hear what she was telling me, I responded to her request in a way that did not enhance our relationship. My official timeline for launching Lisa into adulthood was after she graduated from college and became self-supporting. I told her that I wasn't ready to be her friend. I was adamant about the fact that I was her mother, would always be her mother and, to me, that constituted a hierarchical relationship with me at the top. It was a position of authority that I felt duty bound to assume until she was safely out of the nest.

Lisa on the eve of her wedding, and me on my way to being a parent graduate

At that time, I did not realize that I could become a parent-graduate. Since then, I learned that my parenting role with my first born had already ended. I would take the title of mother with me through life, but the active-parenting role would end. It was time for me to slip out of that role and into the friend role.

When Jamie, my third and last child graduated from college and became self-supporting, I became a parent-graduate,

Class of 1989

Jamie and Betty Anne graduate from Rutgers University on the same day. (Betty Anne becomes a parent - graduate.)

although I didn't realize it at the time. It took me a while to see that my children were all adults and capable of directing their own lives. The parenting role had been a centerpiece of my life for twenty-nine years and it was hard to let it go.

I want to share in the lives of my adult children only when they want me to be with them. I don't want to impose the guilt and fear that I felt from my mother who could find no real purpose for her life after her child-rearing days were over. She could not visualize herself in any other role.

When there are offspring with disabilities, women of worth find the decision about when to become a parent-graduate even more difficult. In my work with the parents of disabled adults, I have observed much fear and guilt around giving up this parenting role, even when the physical demands become overwhelming and cause physical illness for the parent. Mentoring others, on the verge of parent graduation, could be a worthwhile use of our time.

Expanding Roles

If we are to expand our roles, women of worth will have to change from within. Social structures will also have to evolve, in order to accommodate the expanding numbers of women in these new roles. The optimum formula for achieving this is:

> Individual Effort (with assistance)
> + <u>Societal Opportunity</u>
> = Widespread Productive Role Change. [3]

Advocates and organizers for social change can encourage elder women to expand their roles. Reb Zalman's Spiritual Eldering Institute helps elders of both genders change from within and face their elder years with hope instead of despair. This important work can help women of worth evolve both from within and without. This is the important first half of the equation for productive role change.

Women of Worth as Advocates

Incorporating the role of advocate or activist could be a part of every able woman of worth's expanded role concept. Instead of sitting back and complaining about "what the world is coming to," we can all help to bring in the reality of a more caring world.

I saw it in a woman who attended one of my seminars. She had been very quiet during the session and I later learned that she was mourning the recent loss of her husband of thirty-eight years. Since he had been a prominent clergyman she was adjusting to the loss of her role as the minister's wife. When

I spoke with her, I found out that wasn't the only thing that made her quiet. There was a problem in her home community that was causing her much personal pain. As a high school teacher, she experienced great emotional pain with the deaths of several students each year through alcohol-related auto accidents. After we talked about the problem, she began to envision a new, expanded role for herself — as an activist. With the support of the local School Board, she developed a special ceremony to recognize newly licensed drivers and a program to support their safe-driving habits. If we see it as such, role change and expansion can be quite a challenge.

Famous writer and speaker Gloria Steinem shares her findings about women's activism in her ***Outrageous Acts and Everyday Rebellions:***

"Men tend to rebel when young and become more conservative with age, while women tend to be more conservative when young and become rebellious and radical as we grow older. I'd noticed this pattern in the suffragist-abolitionist era, when women over fifty, sixty, and even seventy were a disproportionate number of the activists and leaders — think of Sojourner Truth and Susan B. Anthony, or Elizabeth Cady Stanton and Ida B. Wells — but I assumed it was due to the restrictions placed on younger women by uncontrolled childbirth and a status as household chattel; hard facts that limited all but a few single or widowed white women and all but even fewer free women of color. Yet when I looked at the current wave of feminism, I was surprised to find that the age of self-respecting activism wasn't all that different. The critical mass were still women of thirty, forty, fifty, or beyond — only a decade or so younger than their suffragist counterparts. I realized that most women in their teens and twenties hadn't yet experienced one or more of the great radicalizing events of a woman's life: marrying and discovering it isn't yet an equal (or even nonviolent) institution; getting into the paid labor force and experiencing its limits, from the corporate 'glass ceiling' to the 'sticky floor' of the pink collar ghetto; having children and finding out who takes care of them and who doesn't; and, finally, aging, still the most impoverishing event for women of every race and so potentially the most radicalizing. To put it another way, if young women have a problem, it's only that they think there's no problem." [4]

As I stand at the threshold of elderhood, with Gloria Steinem and millions of other women, I realize that my *shenergy (she-elder energy)* must not be dissipated in time-wasting activities like useless trips to the

Shenergy - the collective energy of third millennial women.

mall. There is an energy crisis around societal cleanup and my shenergy, used properly for me, will give purpose and meaning to my elder years and will be my gift to the future or my planet. For other inspiration and ideas on becoming an activist, read Donna Jackson's book, *How To Make the World a Better Place for Women in Five Minutes a Day*. [5]

Women of Worth as Futurists

Advocates and assertive she-elders are all futurists; in other words, we identify with yet unborn generations. Having a longer view creates a sense of purpose that goes beyond our own lifespans — the important part that continues in the lives and hearts of future generations. Futurists envision a time when a current issue will no longer take valuable shenergy. They will plant trees that they may never see bear fruit.

One of my friends doesn't waste her time wringing her hands about the drug problem in our society. Instead, she goes to a local prison one night each week and spends time with a former drug abuser. This direct action is making a significant difference in her life, which had little meaning after the passing of her beloved husband. It's also having a significant impact on another person whose rehabilitation she supports. This woman of worth is busy clearing fear and re-starting her heart.

Women Behind Bars

Even women serving prison terms and those working within the penal system should find ways to be involved in issues pertinent to them. Women of worth work can be done from prison cells and continued in the outside world, when sentences are commuted or ended. Women, who will age in prison and have no hope of leaving, can become women of worth by addressing issues of importance to them. It is well documented that the inclination toward deviant behavior lessens with age, so the energy that's used for deviance by young woman, can be freed up and put to positive use by older women.

Women Behind Gates

Many women, in the last quarter century, are ensconcing themselves in walled, gated and secured communities. At the same time, the "have-nots" are increasingly becoming victims of crime in their unprotected environments. Perhaps the activist "haves" could spend some shenergy on helping to establish safe communities for those with fewer resources.

Imagine what could happen if the women with resources catch the spirit of the women of worth movement and work toward putting an economic base under all older women. This could be activism at its finest.

Re-Engaged Nurturers

Women of worth from all walks of life can seed the future for the children in their world. Letting a child know he or she is wanted sets the stage for that

child to become a secure adult. A woman-of-worth's unit of time with children is the space between her own memories and the child's knowledge of those memories. Sharing can bring new life to those memories.

Andrews, Julie, Ivan, Bryan, Sabrina and Grammy holding Brent

Nurturing other women of worth can also make for a very satisfying role. My friend Mildred is a wonderful example. Mildred, an only child, never married and spent her young adult life caring for her mother. She spent her later adult life caring for her father and step-mother. After her parents died, Mildred found herself living in a very small studio apartment in a public housing project. Rather than be lonely, she created a new family for herself in the project. She found other senior citizens, who like herself, had little or no family and few resources. She spent time with them each day and checked on them by telephone when she wasn't able to visit. She became Secretary of the local Golden Age Club and started taking bus trips with the group. Although she was retired and lived on a very small pension, she remembered each person's birthday with a card and a call. Mildred will always be, for me, a world-class example of a re-engaged nurturer.

Another re-engaged nurturer told me about the great satisfaction she receives from volunteering at a clinic for AIDS babies. She holds them, rocks them and tells them that they're loved, midwifing their deaths and validating their short lives with love.

Calling Future SEOs

It would be great if the phrase "I'm retired" could be retired. Instead, I wish we could respond to questions about what we're doing in our elder years with, "I'm an advocate," "I'm an activist," "I'm a mediator," "I'm a world-watcher" or "I'm a futurist." In other words, we will have created roles for ourselves that give purpose to our lives and contribute to the future of our communities and the planet.

SEO - a She-Elder Officer is a mature woman who designs and operates her own company that does a piece of the world work of our planet.

As women of worth, we can be the ***SEO (She-Elder Officer)*** of companies of our own design. Within our own companies, we can create roles for ourselves that bring us real satisfaction and allow us to expand into areas unexplored in our previous experience. For careerists, who no longer choose to work a forty-hour week but want to continue working, designing our own companies could bring the sense of purpose and fulfillment we may be missing. Perhaps working a twenty-hour week would keep the careerist in us happy, leaving time to develop other roles we missed earlier.

By using the money our government spends to build just one bomber, we could create a program that provides part-time work, with health benefits and transportation, in pleasant environments, for women of worth careerists who wish to continue to find their primary identity in paid work. This program would put shenergy to work in our world and lessen the poverty experienced by some aging women who are forced to live on insufficient resources.

(1) Ruth Harriet Jacobs, Be An Outrageous Older Woman, Manchester, Connecticut. Knowledge, Ideas & Trends, 1991, pg. 139.
(2) Ruth Harriet Jacobs, Expanding Social Roles for Older Women, Southport, CT: Southport Institute for Policy Analysis. 203-259-8393,
(3) ibid. pg. 24.
(4) Gloria Steinem, Ms. September 1979, pg 64. Republished as "Why Young Women Are More Conservative," in Outrageous Acts and Everyday Rebellions, pg. 211-218.
(5) Donna Jackson, How to Make the World a Better Place for Women in Five Minutes a Day, Hyperion, New York, 1992.

Questions to Ponder About New Roles

1. How many roles have I played in my life?

2. How many roles have been satisfying?

3. What was my favorite role and what made it important?

4. What could I do as a futurist?

5. What could I do as an activist?

6. What roles have I completed and how do I feel about that completion?

7. Envisioning myself as SEO of my own company, how would I describe it?

8. What roles would I like to see for women of worth?

9. How can incarcerated mature women participate in the women of worth movement?

10. How can women dialogue about this sensitive subject and respect each other's opinions?

8. Creativity

I still remember my first needlework. It was a ten-by-ten-inch plastic-framed embroidery of Betsy Ross sewing the first American flag and had the words: "A stitch in time saves nine." My father had taken me to the Betsy Ross house in Philadelphia and, being enchanted by the visit, I decided to do the sampler. I was seven at that time. Following that early needlework, I made beaded hats and handbags for my mother on Mother's day and other special occasions, needlepoint seat covers for our dining room chairs, original doll clothes for my Mary Hoyer doll, crocheted afghans and argyle socks for boyfriends in the nineteen-fifties. Yet, I've never considered myself a creative person through my young adult years.

In our later years, we may have an opportunity to explore our creativity. We may even discover a unique creativity that lay dormant during our earlier years. We may have concentrated our creative abilities in raising our children or in nurturing our career. Or for other reasons, we may not have thought of ourselves as creative as young women. Even if we did think of ourselves as creative, other responsibilities may have left little time for expressing it. We, women of worth, may want to be creative just for the sake of expressing ourselves and seeing what happens.

Here Comes the Shenaissance

How does one live simply, yet creatively? For me this is a question that remains to be explored. Creativity is a

Shenaissance - the third millennium revolution
in art created by women of worth.

gold mine whose treasure can be unearthed with some exploration and work. How can I express the richness that has developed within me, over a lifetime, while letting go of ego? I know there is creativity within me waiting to be released. Is there creativity within you waiting for release? I welcome this dialogue.

"I believe that the most important thing for humankind is our creativity. I also believe that in order to exercise this creativity, people need to be free."[1] This belief is best summed up in the Dalai Lama's words in *Freedom in Exile: The Autobiography of the Dalai Lama* about people needing to be free in order to exercise this creativity. If we have both the creativity within us and the freedom to express it, could we not create a shenaissance?

But who will inspire us? Creative women of worth, with extended healthspans, may have the "freedom" to produce a body of work for the third millennium. They can inspire us. They can be the originators of the shenaissance for the next century. It may be their works that our great-grandchildren enjoy and study. Perhaps we women of worth, of the third millennium, will even live to see future structures erected to house our art.

In thinking about my own creativity, I now see there were several sources of inspiration. When I was a student teacher, in the 1970s, I was blessed with a very talented supervising teacher. She could make anything. When I completed my student teaching, she gifted me with a macrame shoulder bag — a very popular item back then. I have kept that bag with me all these years, because I have always appreciated gifts that someone took time to create for me. It also helps me to remember how she encouraged my creativity by her own modeling.

While I was still a university administrator in the 1980s, I was asked to give a presentation at Stonybrook University on Long Island, New York. This gave me the opportunity to spend an evening with an old friend Adelaide, who lived near the university. Adelaide, in her earlier years, had pioneered some very significant programs for elders. She had also always been involved with the arts, as an avocation, and especially loved to paint in watercolors. Now, in her elder years, she had more time to devote to this avocation. The evening I visited her, she shared with me her initial collection of about a dozen paintings. The colors were radiant and her work truly

A portion of a watercolor by Adelaide Silkworth

inspired. When I asked if she would be willing to sell one of her paintings to me, she was genuinely flattered and offered to give me any one I wanted. The painting I eventually chose is one of my treasures; I spend many pleasurable moments admiring the dancing daffodils in the porcelain vase. Over the years, Adelaide's work became so good that others have asked to study with her. Her work has been featured in many one-woman shows and also in shows that included the work of her students. I am honored to have been her first patron, and hope that maybe my visit gave her added encouragement.

Photo by Elaine Criselone

Judith
Helburn

Even more recently—during the writing of this book— I asked my friend and fellow seminar leader at the Spiritual Eldering Institute, Judith Helburn, to write this chapter, because I didn't think of myself as a creative person. Her writing, which is woven throughout this chapter, is important to me for two reasons. One, she is a very creative woman, having studied the expressive arts of sculpting, jewelry-making and photography. The second reason is the encouragement she gave me to complete this book as it had originally been envisioned with a chapter on creativity. Both her creativity and encouragement inspired me when I needed it.

These, and many other women of worth, have the gift to nurture latent creativity in others. What a blessing that is to the planet. Giving support to another woman of worth may be all that we have to give initially. However, if what goes around comes around, creative women of worth will be there for us when we need them.

But we also need to ask ourselves, how we have expressed our creativity in the past. For those of us who have not considered ourselves very creative, it could be a revelation. How am I expressing my creativity in the present? How would I like to express my creativity in the future?

Color and Clothing

The popular book, **When I Am An Old Woman I Will Wear Purple**, explores the idea of being creative in a way that makes us happy. It's based on the concept that with age, we need answer only to ourselves. We can consciously choose to wear whatever color makes us feel good and be less concerned about impressing others.

For most of my professional life, I wore tailored suits in very conservative colors. That was the uniform for university administrators in my part of the world. There was little room for creativity. I was so busy in these years, that it was actually a relief not to have to think much about what I would wear to work. In some parts of the world, women put on black when they are widowed, and wear black for the rest of their lives. As an administrator, I was not very different from the widow in black. I was following custom.

Now that I am older, however, I have more time and freedom to think about what color can do to help me to express more of my latent creativity. I love color, mainly as accent. I feel good in neutral colors, but I try to add a dash of bright color to each outfit. I'm just beginning my

Joan Ward-Greene and Betty Anne at Conscious Ageing Conference

foray into creative clothing, and really admire women fabric artists, who can create wearable art. I have only recently acquired a few outfits that express different views of my personality.

My sister Joan has a whimsy pin collection. Each of her pins come with a humorous story attached to them. She gives and gets a lot of laughs when she is asked about her pins. I have a clown costume — bright red wig and all — that brings merriment to my life, even as it hangs in my closet. Is creativity with clothing important to you as a woman of worth? It's a question worth pondering.

Self-Portrait

If I were to have my portrait painted, as a woman of worth, how would I portray, on the outside, what was going on in the inside? I recently saw some very interesting portraits of crones. Their costumes were unique and expressed their later-in-life interests and their inner lives. I thought it a very good exercise to think about what I would include in such a portrait. Imagine a museum full of these portraits — for women of the future to view and admire!

Uncovering our Creativity

We, women of worth, can uncover our creativity. In fact, younger women are counting on us to show them the way. Here is what one of Judith's younger friends wrote to her:

> It seems that women, who I know in their fifties, are really themselves and authentic. They have the courage to let their whole selves out and to express fully. They are living as they want to live. They make clear, grounded decisions and change their paths. One incredible woman I met in San Francisco started up a bed and breakfast with her sisters in Wisconsin. It is a special place for quilters, historians and other

special interest groups to meet. She loves it and meets such very interesting people. It is a very satisfying endeavor. She takes off from her work in San Francisco, and uses her computer from afar, so she can run the B & B for one season each year. She finds that making the menus, doing the cooking, and cleaning are fun for her. Her husband misses her but feels her joy.

Another woman, whom I met in Peru, is going into arts management and performance, opening up her creativity. It seems very exciting! She's taking singing lessons, working as a production assistant and loving every moment. She is so alive![2]

To have a younger woman exclaim that an older woman is "so alive," is a real compliment. Giving bloom to our own creative achievement may be as simple as planting a garden of flowers and saying to ourselves, "As these plants grow, so can my creativity. And as these flowers bloom so can I open, petal after petal, exposing myself to more and more creative energy."

We must be willing to dig deeply into the soil of our hidden selves and loosen that soil so that the roots of our creativity can expand and grow. Julia Cameron helps us to do just that in her books *The Artist's Way: A Spiritual Way to Higher Creativity* and *Vein of Gold: A Journey to Your Creative Heart.* The purpose of these books is to assist us in uncovering our hidden life:

> "When I speak of 'Spiritual DNA,' I am talking
> about a stamp of originality that is as definite and
> specific as my blue eyes, blond hair, medium height.
> Just as our physical potentials are encoded at
> conception, it is my belief that we also carry the
> imprint or blueprint of our gifts and their unfolding.
> Often we have far more gifts then we imagine. For
> example, a love of music may indicate a gift for it as
> well. A gift we may not have developed due to the
> circumstances of our birth. Similarly, any voracious
> readers are closet writers, afraid to step into the arena
> of their dreams. This arena, the panoply of a more
> colorful self, is our spiritual DNA, the treasure chest
> we bring into the world and are charged with
> developing."[3]

Cameron, who has been leading workshops in creativity
for years, helps her readers rediscover their creativity through
journaling and writing exercises. She warns the reader that
there will be resistance. That which has been buried for decades does not come unstuck easily. She stresses that it is the
practice, the actual doing of the process, which creates "path-
ways in your consciousness through which the creative forces
can operate."[4] Another great source is Christina Baldwin's
Life's Companion: Journal Writing as a Spiritual Quest.

My friend Judith, didn't consider herself creative until
she was nearly fifty. She comments that, "At that time, I asked
about a dozen friends to give me a small object that could be

put on a treasure necklace, which I would have made for my birthday. A jeweler friend helped me put it together. Because of that necklace, I sold a thriving business and created jewelry for the next eight years." It was as if Judith's horizon has expanded ten-fold. That friend's support added magic to the creative mix in Judith's life.

When Judith began her first class in clay sculpture as a mature adult, she relates that she had the skills of a preschooler and the inhibitions of an adult. After several months, she now says she is probably the equivalent of a third grader in skills and still has a long way to go in learning to take artistic risks. But the growth in her skills and the reduction in her inhibitions continue to delight her. She finds that her sculpting is therapeutic, builds patience and is fun!

How do we discover our creative side? We may not have any idea of where or how to start. We might start by evaluating what we love and appreciate, as Julia Cameron suggests. Is it fine cooking? Is it visiting art galleries? Is it gardening? Reading? A group of she-elders can go through a book on developing creativity together. Having that support could make all the difference.

Celebrations as Creativity

Some women of worth have the gift of celebration. They can turn any event into a party. Birthdays, anniversaries, croning ceremonies and commencements can be enhanced by a celebratory woman of worth. Designing rituals and celebrations is a very creative activity. I am most grateful for people who plan and give parties that are fun and give me pleasant memories to review on less festive days.

I have given a lot of parties over the years, but my favorite was the one designed around my daughter's role as Golda in the musical, "Fiddler On The Roof." It was a delightful theme party, from the invitation to the ethnic food I learned to prepare for the occasion. I was a high school teacher at that time and I used my lunch periods to work with the art teacher to carve a fiddler figure into a rubber tile. He showed me how to use the inked tile to create original invitations. Even now, it brings me great joy to remember how proud I was of Lisa in that role and what a grand party preceded the performance.

For my fifty-fifth birthday party I created a poem that I read to the assembled guests. I recounted that I had experienced my final menstrual period that year. I told of my gratitude for my three children and that I was satisfied with the closing of my womb. I spoke of entering a new phase of my life with much hope. My children, however, were not sure how to react to my sharing of this milestone event at a party. This menopause passage is generally made in silence, but I saw it as an important time in my life and wanted to mark it. This is something new that is happening. Mine is the first generation to mark these passages. I am delighted that more and more croning ceremonies are happening to publicly celebrate this passing from one phase of a woman's life into another.

Creative Memoirs

We know that a good story shares itself. Over the last few years, I have enjoyed reading many books written by women just like me. They helped to enlarge my vision of women in their elder years. Since we are the first wave of women to grow old in large numbers, it is important to tell our stories. We will learn from each other and we can leave a legacy for future generations.

How I wish I could have known my grandmothers, or at least known of their lives. I have little snippets of information about them that does not satisfy my wanting to know more. My paternal grandmother died at age thirty, from pneumonia, leaving six children. My maternal grandmother died at the age of fifty, leaving two daughters in their early twenties. Both grandmothers had lost children through childhood disease. I would like to have known them, if only through the printed word. I would like to have known their hopes and fears.

To have a seven-generation view, we have to go back three generations and forward three generations. I am hoping to live to see three additional generations, perhaps four. I care for myself on all four levels so that this wish can come true.

I have also decided to write my memoirs so that future generations can know of my hopes, fears, successes and failures. The memoirs will also be a way for me to trace my own evolution on the four levels. A few years ago, I wrote my spiritual autobiography while participating in a class at the Unitarian Church in Wellesley, Massachusettes. This writing will form the beginning for my memoirs. I will have to write about the emotional, intellectual and physical levels of my life experience as well. I want to do this soon, before I reach my sixtieth birthday, because the older I get, the more future-oriented I want to be. I do not want to get caught in the past, recounting the same old bromides. So consider, for a moment, the reasons that you may have to pen your own memoirs and what creativity it might unlock.

The Creative Storyteller

My friend Judith collects pictures of older people and pastes them to playing cards for support. Her collection covers the spectrum of moods, places, colors and activities. At seminars, she shares these cards and lets each member of the group select one. Then she tells everyone that they will be creating and telling their own stories about their chosen cards. At this point, there is usually a lot of gasping and worried looks.

She picks a card, holds it up and describes it for those who may not be able to see it well. Then she gives the following instructions: this will be a three-sentence story, but you can make it a little longer if you want. The first sentence will tell who you are in relationship to the picture. In the next sentence, relate what is happening in the picture. And, lastly, tell the results of what happened. Remember, this is pretend, and you can be as outlandish, as dramatic or as unbelievable as you desire. Judith then follows up with a sample story.

Everyone comes up with a great story and realizes how easy it really is to create a story. Try this with some friends, or try a modified version, where each person tells a different story about the same picture.

The Creative Poet

Another favorite exercise of Judith's is the group poem. She hands a piece of paper to a small group of people. She announces a subject, such as crone, wisewoman or wise old man. She instructs everyone to write only one line. Each person passes the paper to the person on the right, who adds another line. This continues until the paper comes back to the first person, who finishes the poem. No one has trouble writing just one line. The following is an example of a group poem:

Crone

It still surprises everyone that I am here,
What's more, the real me isn't sweet and compliant,
How could I be aching from head to toe?
My mind is alive with thoughts of what I still want
    to see and do,
How much I've learned and how much I still do not
    know,
Will I be ready when death beckons?

The poems are read aloud after completion and everyone is pleasantly surprised. The biggest surprise is how easy it was for them to create the group poem. Since she-elder is a new term for a new age of womanhood, it's also interesting to see how we define ourselves. Here is a line poem with some sample lines and verbs with which to play, erase, enlarge and complete.

She-Elder

S   shapes the future
         simplifies her life

_____

H   holds the cosmic field
         handles grief

_____

E   enlarges positive energy
         engages her mind

_____

E   embraces her age
         examines her emotions

_____

L   listens to others
         loves the unlovely

_____

D   develops a new role
         designs her future

_____

E   embodies health
         expands her horizons

_____

R   ritualizes her passages
         responds with hope

_____

The Future Collage

Another way to open up to your creativity is to make a collage about yourself — five years from now. Judith instructs her students to bring old magazines, ribbons and other items small enough to glue onto a posterboard. She suggests that they imagine their ideal self of five years hence. Following a quiet time for reflection, her students create their collages, and then share them to describe who they will be in five years.

For women of worth, the list is endless. Choose your media and let out your creativity. Let yourself flower and flourish. Uncover your creative self. As a women of worth, we owe it to ourselves — and to future generations — to bloom and co-create

(1) The Dalai Lama, *Freedom in Exile: The Autobiography of the Dalai Lama.* San Francisco, Harper, 1990. p. 242.
(2) Joyce Lozito in an e-mail, 1998.
(3) Julia Cameron, *The Vein of Gold: A Journey to Your Creative Heart.* New York: G.P. Putnam's Sons, 1996. p. 5.
(4) Julia Cameron, *The Artist's Way: A Spiritual Path to Higher Creativity.* New York: Penguin, 1992. p. xiii.

Questions to Ponder About Creativity

1. Is there creativity, within me, waiting for release?

2. How have I expressed my creativity in the past?

3. How am I expressing my creativity now?

4. How would I like to express my creativity in the future?

5. How can I express myself with color?

6. What would my self-portrait be like?

7. Is dressing creatively important to me?

8. What can I do to uncover my creativity?

9. Why would I wish to write my memoirs?

10. What three-sentence story can I create from a selected picture?

9. The Great Shift

The millennial shift toward a vision of the importance of feminine wisdom has already begun. It lives within the psyches of those of us who have lived long enough to have experienced significant change and know that still more significant change lies ahead. Unlike previous visions, this new vision will include seasoned women in large numbers. The vision has been building slowly for the last quarter century and is now being voiced by women throughout the world. Is it time to add your voice to the present and your vision to the future?

Visionaries

I believe as women of worth, we must be conscious in the present moment and planning for the future. I have written this book partly because I wanted to take the time to consciously examine my responsibilities for the future. But, secondly, I wanted to share my questions and open a dialogue with other women of worth who are seeking support for their personal and planetary visions. I feel such optimism —this is *Polly-elder* speaking now, not Pollyanna—for what can be accomplished through the spiritual eldering movement. I want to be one of the vital women of worth of the third millennium. I want to experience this with other women of worth who are also future-oriented.

Polly-elder - a seasoned woman with a realistic view of life, who can remain positive and make a contribution to the planet.

Reb Zalman has said, "I came to that place where I woke up. It made me take responsibility for who I will become tomorrow." Awakening to the task of taking responsibility for who we will become tomorrow can lay the foundation for creating purposefulness in our lives.

Women of worth visionaries can be a blessing.

Avoiding Shut Down

If your internal software tells you at a certain age or stage to shut down your life and go into retirement, you may need some re-programming. It won't be time to shut down until the end of your healthspan is near. You still have a lot of living to do.

A great example is Reb Zalman. In his seventh decade of life, he learned about the texture of elder time and how to use it to better serve his life and the planet. He knows that his body works better at certain hours of the day, so he schedules his most demanding work during those hours. He is conscious of his energy flow. He is conscious of when it needs to be recharged. From his example, I have learned how to re-program my spiritual, intellectual, emotional and physical energy to continue to avoid the premature shut down virus that's rampant in our elder culture.

In her book *New Passages: Mapping Your Life Across Time*, Gail Sheehy tells us that it's useful to look ahead to the most vital women of age and see how they have met the challenges of later-life passages. Cecelia Hurwich, one of the participants in the Esalen conference conducted a study on women in their seventies, eighties and nineties for her doctorate at the Center for Psychological Studies in Albany, California.[1] What were their secrets?

"They live very much in the present, but they always have plans for the future," Dr. Hurwich said. They had mastered the art of "letting go" of their egos gracefully so they could concentrate their attention on a few fine-tuned priorities. They continued to live in their own homes, but involved themselves in community or worldly projects that they found of consuming interest. Close contact with nature was important to them, as was maintaining a multigenerational network of friends. And as they grew older, they found themselves concerned more with feeding the soul than the ego. Surprisingly, these zestful women were not in unusually good physical shape. They had their fair share of the diseases of age— arthritis, loss of hearing, impaired vision— but believing they still had living to do, they concentrated on what they could do rather than on what they had lost.

Over the ten-year course of the study, most were widowed. This hardship, like so many others they had endured during their lives, they turned into a source of growth rather than defeat. Frequently, they mentioned in conversation, "After my husband's death I learned to..." [2]

One of the things we can learn to do is to use shenergy and time differently.

Women of Worth on the Move

Women of worth are rising up around the world. Although not formally organized at this time, we know that there are issues of importance we will address individually and others that require group support.

The spiritual eldering movement is a grass-roots event. It is growing in the heads and hearts of women worldwide. A movement is composed of people moving. To feel its warmth and excitement around us is empowering. We know that we are seeding the future with very wholesome ideas that may bear fruit in the third millennium.

Incompletes

Women of worth can learn to fold her past into the present and the present into the future. This gives us intergenerational thinking, perhaps spanning as many as seven generations. If we are fortunate, we can look back at the three generations that preceded us and may know the three generations that follow. When we look closely at the lives of those family members, who have come before us, we know whether they finished their lives satisfactorily or received an "incomplete."

One way we are beginning to understand more about life completion is from the writings of Brian Weiss. In his book entitled **Many Lives, Many Masters**, he speaks about receiving very personalized messages from very spiritual sources, which he calls "the Masters:" "The implications were overwhelming. The light after death and the life after death; our choosing when we are born and when we will die; the sure and unerring guidance of the Masters; life times measured in lessons learned and tasks fulfilled, not in years; charity, hope, faith, and love; doing without expectations of return — this knowledge was for me." [4] If we have not learned our lessons, we too will get "incompletes."

What are we sent here to accomplish?

I have been working on that question for several years. I believe that I was sent here to be a conciliator — to reduce prejudice and encourage understanding of differences. My life choices have allowed me to participate in this process. The decisions that I have made just felt "right" at the time. Having been drawn to the work of the Spiritual Eldering Institute and the trans-denominational spirit of the Spiritual Eldering movement, I feel part of a larger destiny group. I feel that I have come to earth for such a time as this. You probably have, too.

Time

Women of worth time is precious. There is much to be learned and much to accomplish. When I hear from a friend that she has just returned from the local shopping mall with items that, by her own admission, she does not need and will have difficulty storing, I am greatly saddened by this misuse of elder time.

On the other hand, when I call my friend Elizabeth and she tells me that she has just spent time supporting a young man through a troubled time in his life, I am encouraged. Or when I speak with Steffi, who is giving Yoga classes at the local Senior Center, I am also encouraged. These women have learned to make their days count and pass them in ways that make a contribution to their world.

Learning Communities

Part of the agenda for any woman of worth will be to determine what lesson she was sent here to learn and whether or not she'll complete that lesson. This is important lifework, which must be done as part of the life-completion process.

Margaret Mead, one of the wise women of the twentieth century, told us that, "If this society is going to survive it is a question of citizen volunteer associations and ongoing teaching-learning communities empowering each other."

By forming women of worth learning communities, we can focus our shenergy on learning what we must learn individually and also on the larger lessons to be learned for the planet. According to Reb Zalman, "We suffer from the cancer of opaqueness and we need dyadic work with strangers." It must be strangers because they can see us as we are now — not for what we have been. So it may be that we need to dialogue in new groups with those who are meeting as women of worth for the first time.

Sage-ing Centers

The concept of a Sage-ing Center, a community organization for the third millennium, is beginning to take form. The purposes for this organization would be: to raise the consciousness of elders on all four levels; promote inter-generational learning; and help spiritual elders to stay connected to the future.

Some community organizations, that have served society well in the second millennium, will continue into the new millennium. Other

Sage-ing Centers - programs designed to assist spiritual elders with their life completion work.

organizations, that have isolated and divided elders, will need to be revisioned or eliminated.

In *Little Gidding,* T.S. Elliot talks about reaching an intersection of time and space with eternity. Here he meets a stranger who urges him to let go of all thoughts and theories he has been taught in the past, for they have served their purpose and he must await a new language for the time ahead. Perhaps we, too, have come to an intersection of time and space and need a new language and new structures for the time ahead. (See the list of neologisms in the appendix.)

In the new millennium spiritual elders, in significant numbers, will leave the sidelines and be mainstreamed into world culture. They will choose to add their energy to the millennial shift rather than replicate outdated models of aging. The mainstreaming of elders is exciting and inevitable. To be a hope-holder is to truly believe that we can experience our greatest personal fulfillment in elderhood. That kind of thinking pulls us into the future.

A team of spiritual elders is developing a curriculum that will be a new model to ennoble the process of aging. It will be taught in inter-generational and trans-denominational Sage-ing Centers around the world. These centers will be ongoing teaching-learning communities.

3 Ms

When primitive she-elders gathered around stone circles in Ireland and England, sharing secrets of healing and drawing energy from electrically active crystal in the stones, they had no means of communication with other such circles on the planet.

We third millennials (3Ms) have global communication at our keyboards and a much wider space in our hearts for spiritual diversity. As futurists, we will make the connections, in the first century of the third millennium and the planet will feel the shift.

The Spiritual Elderarchy

When Judaic-Christian spiritual elders, metaphorically speaking, stand again at Sinai in the third millennium they will be able to revision the ten commandments. They will speak of them, and other such guides to world wisdom, in a new language that will address an equality of spirit within homo-sapiens.

As sages-in-training, we can help to blend the patriarchies and matriarchies of historical cultures into a spiritual elderarchy . This equality of spirit will enable us to better understand the issues of the earlier periods of our personal and collective histories in which gender and societal expectations colored our world views. The great millennial shift will happen as a result of this blending and

Spiritual Elderarchy - mature men and women of worth, living consciously on all four levels, working together as equals, engendering respect for their world work for future generations.

focusing of elder energy for the first time in recorded history. The spiritual elderarchy will create energy to support our world-work and enable us to leave loving legacies for the future.

The Penultimate Passage

As elders we have some very important choices to make. One of those choices is to decide if we will become a spiritual elder. This will take work but it will be work at our own pace. Because of our extended lifetimes we will have the opportunity to make the penultimate passage into spiritual elderhood. If we cherish this opportunity, and do our inner-elder and outer-elder work, we will surely evolve as spiritual elders, women of worth.

(1) Cecelia Hurwich, "Vital Women in Their Eighties and Nineties: A Longitudinal Study," Dissertation, University of California, Berkley. Available through Dissertation Services in Ann Arbor, Michigan, order #LD01950.
(2) Gail Sheehy, *New Passages: Mapping Your Life Across Time.* New York: Random House, Inc., 1995 pg. 414
(3) Brian Weiss, *Many Lives, Many Masters.* New York: Simon & Schuster Inc: New York. 1988, pg 87.

Questions to Ponder on
The Great Shift

1. What kind of woman-of-worth shift am I experiencing?

2. How can I take responsibility for the person I will become tomorrow?

3. What can I learn from the vital women in Cecelia Hurwich's study?

4. If I could create my ideal she-elder life, what would it be like?

5. What work must I do to get a "complete" by the end of my life journey?

6. What organizations in my community have become obsolete?

7. What new language and structures would I design for the future?

8. Do I have a seven-generation concept of time?

9. What will be my gift for the betterment of the planet?

10. What will be new about me in the new millennium?

The Spiritual Eldering Institute

Dr. Zalman Schachter-Shalonii founded the Spiritual Eldering Institute in 1988 and continues to inspire its growth. His landmark book *From Age-ing to Sage-ing: A Profound New Vision of Growing Older* forms the theoretical foundation for of the Spiritual Eldering Institute. The non-profit educational institute currently provides training for seminar leaders, workshops throughout the United States and Europe and spiritual eldering resources.

For additional information contact:

Spiritual Eldering Institute
970 Aurora Avenue
Boulder, CO 80302
303-449-SAGE
e-mail info@spiritualeldering.org
www.spiritualeldering.org

Dr. Betty Anne Sullivan-Szuts
Certified Sage-ing Seminar Leader
14311 Champions Drive
Houston, TX 77069
291-895-0321
e-mail bettyanne.ivan@sbcglobal.net

Neologisms
New Words and Expressions for a New Millenium.

Spiritual Elderarchy - mature men and women of worth, living consciously on all four levels, working together as equals, engendering respect for their world work for future generations.

Gold Collar - symbol for raising the collective value of mature women on the planet.

Herstory - the documentation of the work of women of all ages in the last century of the second millennium and the first century of the third millen-nium.

Herstorical Period - forming in the last century of the second millennium and gaining momentum in the first century of the third millennium.

Mother of Sheriatrics - a woman, who will rise to global prominence, and place post-menopausal women's medical issues on the world agenda.

Polly-elder - a seasoned woman with a realistic view of life, who can remain positive and make a contribution to the planet.

SEO - a She-Elder Officer is a mature woman who designs and operates her own company that does a piece of the world work of our planet.

Sharmony - the result of a conscious mind move to do world work in a harmonious group of women.

She-Elder - a post-menopausal woman, living consciously on all four levels of her being, who is
future-oriented, contributing to world work and
otherwise self-defining.

She-Elder Archetype - in process and may take a
milleniumn to form.

She-Elder Enriched - the state of the planet when
receiving the positive energy from women of
worth.

She-Elder Stateswoman - a woman who will open
physical and symbolic doors and encourage the
emergence of she-elders in the third millennium.
Like Maggie Kuhn, she will go right to the top to
facilitate change.

She-Elder Valuation - a concept needing definition in
the third millennium.

Shenergy - the collective energy of third millennial
women.

Shenaissance - the third millennium revolution in art
created by women of worth.

Shentellect - the critical mass of intellectual capital
created by mature, educated women of worth.

Woman of Worth - a post-menopausal woman with an
important role, of her own design, who will
positively impact the planet.

Selected Reading List
for She-Elders In The Third Millennium

Anne Bancroft. *Weavers of Wisdom: Women Mystics of the Twentieth Century.* Hammondsworth, England: Arkana, 1989.

Joan Borysenko. *Fire in the Soul: A New Psychology of Spiritual Optimism.* New York:Warner Books, 1993.

Lydia Bronte. *The Longevity Factor.* New York: Harper Perennial, 1993

Barbara Ann Brennan. *Light Emerging: The Journal of Personal Healing.* New York: Bantam, 1993.

Paula Brown Doriss and Diana Lasken Siegal. *Ourselves Growing Older: Women Aging with Knowledge and Power.* Simon & Schuster, 1987. revised edition, 1994.

Robert Butler, MD. and Myrna Lewis. *Love and Sex after Sixty, Revised Edition.* New York:Ballentine Books, 1993.

Deepak Chopra. *Ageless Body, Timeless Mind: The Quantum Alternative to Growing Old.* New York: Harmony Books, 1993.

Deepak Chopra. *The Seven Spiritual Laws of Success.* San Rafael, CA: Amber-Allen Publishing, 1993.

Tom Cole. *The Journey of Life: A Cultural History of Aging in America.* Cambridge University Press, 1992.

Larry Dossey. *Healing Words.* San Francisco: Harper Collins, 1993.

Ann E Gerike, Ph.D. and Peter Kohlsaat. *Old is Not a Four-Letter Word.* Papier-Mache Press, Watsonville, CA, 1997.

Connie Goldman and Rebecca Mahler. *Secrets of Becoming a Late Bloomer: Extraordinary People on the Art of Staying Creative, Alive, and Aware in Mid-Life and Beyond.* New York, Still Point Publishing, 1995.

Ruth Harriet Jacobs, Ph.D. *Be an Outrageous Older Woman: A R-A-S-P (Remarkable Aging Smart Person).* Connecticut: Knowledge, Ideas & Trends, 1991.

Maggie Kuhn. *No Stone Unturned: The Life and Times of Maggie Kuhn.* With Christina Long & Laura Quinn. Ballentine Books: New York, 1991.

Sandra Haldman Martz, Ed. *When I am an Old Woman I Shall Wear Purple.* Papier-Mache Press, Watsonville, CA., 1987.

Patricia Monaghan. *The Book of Goddesses and Heroines.* St. Paul, MN: Llewellyn Publications, 1993.

Thomas Moore. *Care of the Soul.* New York: Harper Perennial, 1992.

Caroline Myss, Ph.D. *Anatomy of the Spirit.* New York: Harmony Books, 1996.

Caroline Myss, Ph.D. *Why People Don't Heal and How They Can.* New York: HarmonyBooks, 1997.

Christiane Northrup, M.D. *Women's Bodies, Women's Wisdom.* New York: Bantam Books, 1994.

Jane Porcino, Ph.D. *Living Longer, Living Better.* New York: The Continuum Publishing Company, 1991.

George Sheehan. *Personal Best: The Foremost Philosopher of Fitness Shares Techniques and Tactics for Success and Self-Liberation.* Emmaus, PA: Rodale Press, 1989.

George
Sheehan

Gail Sheehy. *New Passages: Mapping Your Life Across Time.*
New York: Random House, 1995.

Diane Stein. *Casting the Circle: A Woman's Book of Ritua*l.
Freedom, CA: Crossing Press, 1992.

Gloria Steinem. *Revolution From Within: A Book of Self-
Esteem.* Boston: Little Brown and Co., 1993.

Gloria Steinem. *Moving Beyond Words/ Age, Rage, Sex, Power,
Money, Muscles: Breaking the Boundaries of Gender.*
New York, Touchstone Books, 1995.

Alexandra Stoddard. *Living A Beautiful Life.* New York: Avon
Books, 1986.

Barbara Walker. *The Woman's Encyclopedia of Myths and
Secrets.* New York: Harper and Row, 1983.

Zalman Schachter-Shalomi, Ronald S. Miller. *From Age-ing to
Sage-ing: A Profound NewVision of Growing Older.* New
York: Warner Books, Inc., 1995.

Symbols

3Ms 145

A

Academy for Jewish Religion 82
Adelaide 125
Advocate 112
Alan 90
Albright, Madeline 24
Allopathic medicine 47
American Society of Plastic and
     Reconstructive Sur 44
Anand, Margo 36
Angelou, Maya 24
Anthony, Susan B. 116
Aristotle 24
Art of Sexual Ecstasy: The Path of
     Sacred Sexualit 36
Asclepiades of Bethynia 45
Assertive women 112
Association of Theological Schools 83

B

Bahira 35
Baldwin, Christina 130
Be An Outrageous Older Woman 110
Body Language 28
Body Talk 39
Brain Builders 57
Bruteau, Beatrice 69
Buddha 24, 95, 97

C

Cameron, Judith 129
Careerist 112
Catholic 54, 90, 91, 98
Center for Psychological Studies,
     Albany, CA 141
Chum networker 112
Confuscious 24
Congregation Beth Shalom 82
Congregationalist 91
Conscious Aging Conference 29, 51
Cornelia, Grandaunt 95
Cosmetics On The Body 44
Crone 106, 135
Crone, The 51

D

Dalai Lama 124
Douglass College 158
Dreyfus, Rabbi Ellen 82

E

Elizabeth 5, 43, 95, 143
Elliot, T.S. 145
Emotional Flow 74
Emotional Intelligence 69
Escapist 112

F

Faded beauties 112
Florence 29
Freidan, Betty 24
From Age-ing to Sage-ing: A Profound New
     Vision of Growing Older 12, 149
Frontier thinking 53
Future Collage 137

G

Gaia 92
Goddess Re-awakening 69
Golden Age Club 120
Greeley, Andrew 54
Grey Panthers 111

H

Heilbrun, Caroline 75
Helburn, Judith 126
Herstorical period 21
Herstory 20
High Sex 36, 37
Hitting The Wall 64
Holmes, John 76
Hormone Replacement Therapy (HRT) 41
Houston, Jean 24
How To Make the World a Better Place for
     Women in Five Minutes a Day 117
Hugs 34
Hurwich, Cecilia 140-1, 148

I

J

K

L

M

N

O

P

Q

R

About the Author

Betty Anne Sullivan has been actively involved with trans-denominational work for over forty years. She is passionately committed to building bridges of understanding between members of differing spirit expressions.

She holds a Bachelor's of Science degree from Douglass College in New Brunswick, New Jersey, a Master of Education degree and a Doctor of Education degree in Administration from Rutgers University in New Brunswick, New Jersey. After raising her three children to school age, Betty Anne began her career as a high school home economics teacher focusing on foods and nutrition. She also began the program "living with children," which is an inter-generational experience. When the first group of mainstreamed mentally-challenged students entered the high school she developed a curriculum to meet their needs.

Betty Anne has served as a high school vice-principal in two high schools, a New Jersey State Supervisor of Education and a university administrator. She has held district, county, state, university and regional positions. Her Rutgers University directorships included: the ModelNetics Management Training Program for school administrators; the Northeast Network for Curriculum Coordination; and in-service teacher education. As a visiting professor at Georgian Court College, Lakewood, New Jersey she supervised student teachers across the curricula. Betty Anne has been involved with model programs throughout her career in education.

She became interested in the education of mature adults and accepted the directorship of the Suffolk County

Respite Care Program in Suffolk County, New York.
While in that position, she worked with members of the
Alzheimer's research faculty at Stonybrook University, in
Stonybrook, New York and the gerontology faculty at
Long Island University, Southampton, New York where
she taught *Health and Aging* to graduate students.

Dr. Sullivan directed the Gerontology Program at
Union County College in Cranford, New Jersey where
she taught *The Psychology of Aging and The Sociology
of Aging.* As a visiting professor at Wheaton College,
Norton, Massachusetts she taught *Aging in America* .

Betty Ann is a certified biblical studies teacher from
the Bethel Institute, Madison, Wisconsin. She has four
decades of experience teaching the old and new testament.

Betty Anne developed the first leader's training curriculum for the Spiritual Eldering Institute and served on
the Board of Directors. She is one of the original eight
seminar leaders and has conducted Spiritual Eldering seminars for the past five years. Her seminars open a sacred
space that enable participants to use their elder-power for
spiritual and social transformation. She encourages elders everywhere to share in the joy of becoming a spiritual elder.

Betty Anne lives in Houston, Texas with her husband
Ivan Szuts. They have a blended family of five children
and five grandchildren who live in Wellesley, Massachusetts; Hightstown, New Jersey; San Francisco, California; Bend, Oregon; and Kitchener, Ontario. Ivan and Betty
Anne enjoy traveling to see their far-flung family and bless
e-mail for stimulating communication.

If you would like to have a seminar in your community
or receive a schedule of forthcoming seminars you may reach
Betty Anne through e-mail at basullivan@bigcity.net.

ORDER FORM

To order more copies of

Spiritual Elders — Women of Worth in the Third Millennium

mail copies of this form with your check to:

Betty Anne Sullivan-Szuts
14311 Champions Drive
Houston TX 77069

Spiritual Elders:
Women of Worth In The Third Millennium
To purchase from the author
send $13.50 (Book $10 + Shipping & Handling)

The book is also available from:

$ Amazon.com
  $15.95 + Shipping & Handling

Ship to:

Name _____

Address _____

Address _____

 City, State, Zip _____

Phone (   ) _____

Special Instruction: _____

_____

_____